D0981821

The Best Defense

The Best Defense

TRUE STORIES OF INTENDED VICTIMS
WHO DEFENDED THEMSELVES WITH A FIREARM

Robert A. Waters

CUMBERLAND HOUSE
NASHVILLE, TENNESSEE

Copyright © 1998 by Robert A. Waters

All rights reserved. Written permission must be secured from
the publisher to use or reproduce any part of this work, except
for brief quotations in critical reviews or articles.

Published by Cumberland House Publishing, Inc.,
431 Harding Industrial Drive, Nashville, TN 37211.

Cover design by Unlikely Suburban Design
Text design by Joel Wright

Scripture quotations are from THE NEW KING JAMES VERSION of
the Bible. Copyright © 1979, 1980, 1982,
Thomas Nelson, Inc., Publishers.

Library of Congress Cataloging-in-Publication Data

Waters, Robert A., 1944–
    The best defense : true stories of intended victims who
defended themselves with a firearm / Robert A. Waters.
        p.   cm.
    ISBN 1-888952-97-0 (pbk. : alk. paper)
    1. Firearms—United States—Use in crime prevention—
Case studies.   2. Self-defense—Case studies.   I. Title
HV7431.W38   1998
363.3'3'0973—dc21   98-28692
                                                            CIP

Printed in the United States of America

2 3 4 5 6 7 8 — 03 02 01 00 99

Dedicated to my brother, John T. Waters Jr. It is a cliché to say that this book would not have been written without you. But it's true. Thanks for the encouragement through the years and for being there when the chips were down.

In Memoriam
Kenneth Moring
R.I.P.

Contents

Acknowledgments

A special thanks to my agent, Rhonda J. Winchell of The Author's Agency. You sold the book that wasn't supposed to sell.

Thanks to Ron Pitkin, president of Cumberland House Publishing, for taking a chance on an unpublished author. The assistance of your staff in guiding me through the publishing of this book is appreciated. Special mention must be made of Mary Beth Trask, Lori McNeese, and Lisa Taylor.

The following would-be victims made themselves available for long interviews, or took the time to write down their recollections. I cannot thank them enough. They are: Rick Amoedo; Gary Baker; Paul Brite; Jim Eichelberg; Marion County, Florida, Sheriff Ken Ergle; Sammie Foust; the late Kenneth Moring; Mary Ellen Moring; Frances Postlethwait; Fred Prasse; Travis Dean Neel; Amanda Whaley Shaw; Doug and Judy Stanton; Sam Turrisi; and Rodney Whaley. Obviously, without your cooperation, this book would never have been written. Others spoke to me in confidence—you know who you are, and how much I appreciate your views.

I am grateful to Marilyn, my wife of twenty-five years, who encouraged me to take early retirement so that I could pursue my dream to be a writer. You took over most of the financial burden of our household while I wrote, and I thank you for your continued love and support.

Thanks to my son, Sim, for the never-ending photo shoots as we searched to find a presentable photograph of the author. And I'm grateful to LeAnn for being supportive of a distracted father bent on writing a book and for brow-beating all your friends into buying a copy.

Thanks to my father, John T. Waters, for years of showing your children ethics-in-action. Kim, thanks for always being supportive. Zack, you've been an unwavering confidant from the beginning. Thanks.

I value the friendship of Fran, Dot, and Glenn Moore. When you gave me a subscription to the National Rifle Association, you regenerated an idea that had lain dormant for many years. Thanks so much for your generosity over the years.

Finally, to all my friends and fellow-laborers at the Central Church of Christ in Ocala, Florida: I love you all. In these accounts, good triumphs over evil. But righteousness doesn't always prevail. If we keep our faith, however, we will conquer even death.

Preface

On December 8, 1994, 74-year-old Lillie Mae Ponder returned home from church to find that her house had been burglarized. She lived near the crime-ridden Ivey Lane housing project in Orlando, Florida, and kept a .38 Special for protection. Just hours later, while she and her husband, Paul, were asleep, the burglar returned. When the Ponders awoke and confronted the intruder, he sprayed them with Mace. Nearly blinded, Lillie Mae reached into a drawer and pulled out her gun. She fired, hitting him in the cheek and killing him instantly.

She later said she was afraid for the life of her husband, who was confined to a wheelchair.

Police called it a "lucky shot." They also called it a classic case of self-defense.

•••

Perry and Debra Jones were sleeping in their Waller, Texas, home on the night of December 11, 1995, when a burglar broke their bedroom window.

Wearing black clothes, a camouflage mask, and surgical gloves, he climbed into the Joneses' bedroom. Perry Jones awoke and shouted for the man to leave. When he refused, Jones picked up a shotgun that lay beside his bed and fired, fatally wounding the intruder.

Because self-defense using firearms is usually a local event, it is one of the least known issues in America today. No single story is enough to make national news. When examined collectively, however, these accounts show that a significant number of Americans are choosing to fight back when attacked. On January 31, 1996, after grocer Sam Turrisi killed an armed robber in his store, the *Orlando Sentinel* reported that the robber was "the ninth gunman in eighteen months to die at the hands of an intended victim" in Orange County, Florida.

There are conflicting estimates of the number of individuals who successfully use guns to defend themselves and others. Neither police departments nor the federal government keep such statistics. Gary Kleck, a criminologist at Florida State University, has done extensive research into all forms of gun violence. In his widely acclaimed 1991 book, *Point Blank: Guns and Violence in America,* Kleck estimates that there are between 400,000 and 500,000 uses of firearms each year for defensive purposes. In recent years, his research has indicated that there may be up to 2.5 million instances of self-defense with firearms annually.

The vast majority of these confrontations do not end in violence—usually a potential victim merely shows a gun and an aggressor retreats, as happened in the case of Denver's notorious "Ski Mask Rapist."

Since the summer of 1985, this unknown rapist had been terrorizing the city. His method of operation was to stalk single women, determine the nights they would be home alone, and break into their homes after they had gone to bed. He always wore a ski mask and gloves, and cut their outside telephone lines. Once the attacker had isolated his victim, he would brutally rape her, often for hours. The police were stumped as to his identity.

On January 4, 1986, all had gone according to plan for the rapist. He stood over the bed of his intended victim, erotic fantasies playing in his mind. Rape quickly became an afterthought, however, when the victim suddenly sat up and pointed a pistol between his eyes. The intruder dove through the kitchen window. Investigating officers found that, as in the other cases, the telephone lines had been cut. It took two years, but a task force finally captured Frank Vargas. During that time, the Ski Mask Rapist had violated twenty women. He had been thwarted once, by an armed woman.

• • •

My purpose for writing this book is not to enter the gun control debate, but to recount dramatic true stories of split life-or-death decisions made by innocent victims defending themselves, their families, their employees, or strangers.

While scanning local newspapers, which is where such stories are often reported, I came across thousands of such cases.

From the February 11, 1995, *Atlanta Constitution:* A shooting was videotaped by a store camera at the Lakewood Grocery Store in Atlanta. The store owner, a Korean immigrant, was stocking shelves when a man entered, apparently scoping the place. The owner's wife was behind the counter. The man left, but returned a few minutes later with an accomplice. They pulled out pistols and attempted to rob the clerk, whereupon the grocer pulled his own gun, fired, and killed one of the robbers. At the time the newspaper reported the story, the police were still searching for the second robber.

From the February 7, 1995, *Orlando Sentinel:* Around midnight, two men broke into the apartment of Raymond Scott. Scott, asleep in his bedroom, was awakened by strange noises coming from the living room. He cracked the door and saw a masked intruder tying up his two adult children with black electrical tape. Scott burst into the living room, firing his 9 mm handgun. A second intruder began shooting at him. After a wild gunfight, both attackers ran from the apartment, and Scott called police. Home invasion is a current fad among central Florida criminals, but it didn't pay for the two who broke into Scott's apartment. Stephen LeRoy Jones was arrested while being treated for gunshot wounds at the Orlando Regional Medical Center. His partner, Shonrell J. Harper, wasn't so lucky. At 7:30 the following morning, he was found dead under a stairway in Scott's apartment complex. A ski mask and a roll of electrical tape were found with his body.

From the December 12, 1995, *Mountain Press,* Prather, California: A woman ran into a local church for protection from an attacker. The pastor hid her in a back room, then came out and tried to reason with the assailant. The man didn't want to listen, however, and opened fire. Shot in the hand, the pastor ran to his office and slammed the door shut. The gunman broke through the door, at which time the pastor shot him between the eyes, killing him instantly.

From the June 10, 1995, *Gastonia Observer*, Gastonia, North Carolina: A young woman walked alone outside a mall, trailed by a trio of men with violent pasts. One had served hard time on three occasions. When the men continued to threaten the woman, a bystander, Christopher Gore, intervened. The three-time loser, who had consumed vast quantities of beer that day, pulled a gun and began shooting at Gore. The samaritan pulled his own 9 mm handgun and returned fire, killing the felon.

As stated previously, in most instances of self-defense, the attacker is not killed, but merely captured or run off. In October 1995, a Griswold, Connecticut, woman telephoned her brother to tell him that someone was trying to break into her house. Her brother called police and raced to the scene. By the time he got there, the woman was holding the suspect, a teenage burglar, with a .22 rifle. Police quickly arrived and captured three accomplices nearby.

It is a general misconception that the police exist to protect the public. This is true only in the most generic sense—i.e., once a criminal act is committed, and a suspect caught and convicted, theoretically he is locked up so that he cannot prey on other people. The problem is that someone has to be a victim before the criminal can be taken out of society. And many offenders commit dozens of violent acts before they are caught. This doesn't even take into account the fact that the criminal justice system continually releases the most violent offenders.

Since police are unable to protect citizens from violent attacks, many individuals feel that it is their own responsibility to protect themselves and their families.

All states have laws governing and restricting the right of self-defense. Florida law states, "The use of force is justifiable when a person is resisting any attempt to murder such person or to commit a felony upon him or in any dwelling house in which person shall be." Such wording is open to interpretation.

After two incidents in which homeowners shot intruders, one central Florida sheriff interpreted the law this way: "In your home, you have a right to protect every square inch of it. . . . When criminals break into a home, they better be prepared to pay the ultimate price."

Other Florida law enforcement officials have attempted to be more restrictive, but public pressure has usually prevailed, and home owners and business owners who have shot intruders have almost always been found to have been legally justified.

For example, on November 14, 1992, Manny Roman, a Cuban refugee who owned Aries Auto Repair in Miami, was spending the night at his shop. He was armed because the place had been plagued with break-ins. At about 1:30 A.M., he heard a window break. Moments later he heard someone rummaging about in his office. Roman grabbed his Beretta 9 mm semiautomatic. As he explained, "When I opened the door, we were face to face. I was afraid. I just kept shooting and I went back and closed the door of the office and dialed 911." Police found Stanley Dixon, a crack addict, with eleven bullet holes in his body. A hammer was grasped in his hand.

Police initially stated that Roman would not be arrested. Eight months later, however, the state charged him with murder. Kathleen Fernandez Rundle, the County State Attorney, claimed that Roman was "lying in wait" for the next person to break into his shop. For that reason, she stated, he had "entrapped" Dixon. Roman replied that the reason he was in his shop late at night was because he had worked until late in the evening and was too exhausted to drive to his home across town.

Rundle also said that reloading his weapon after the shooting showed premeditation. The business owner advised her that he'd reloaded when he heard other noises outside.

The community was outraged at the state attorney's decision to charge Roman. Under intense public pressure, Rundle approached Roman on two occasions, asking him to accept plea bargains with no jail time. He refused. He later said, "I knew I had done the right thing in protecting my life."

On November 3, 1995, the Dade County State Attorney's Office reluctantly dropped all charges after a sixteen-member grand jury refused to indict Roman. After the finding, Rundle said, "I have concluded that it is extremely unlikely that a Dade County jury would convict him."

Most states recognize that if a citizen's life, or that of another, is in danger from a criminal attack, a citizen has the right to take every measure available to save his or her own life or the life of another.

The "home protection" law in Tennessee, for instance, has changed little since it was written at the time of Cherokee Indian attacks on settlers in the early 1800s. It consists of two subjective tests: "apprehension," or a sense of impending danger; and "external manifestations": Was the intruder armed? Was he under the influence of mind-altering substances? Did he have a prior record?

New York's self-defense law is one of the most restrictive in the nation, as exemplified by the following incident. In February 1996, Timothy Pastuck saw his neighbor being brutally attacked with a baseball bat. Pastuck grabbed his unlicensed .22 rifle and shouted for the attacker to stop. When he refused, Pastuck shot him three times, wounding the assailant and driving him off.

The police called Pastuck a hero but arrested him anyway. He was charged with attempted murder, assault with a deadly weapon, and unlawful possession of a weapon. He spent a full day in jail, trying to bail himself out as the public railed against a policy that would not allow a citizen to protect another person in danger of being murdered.

Pastuck was forced to appear in court, where the district attorney, under intense public pressure, finally dropped all charges. Pastuck said, "You try to do the right thing, and the next thing you know you're in the system." Then, obviously confused, he stated, "I don't know what they want; people, citizens to react, don't react."

The stories in this book portray citizens who did react. Citizens such as Travis Dean Neel. Just outside the Houston, Texas, city limits, on January 21, 1994, Neel watched as Harris County Deputy Frank Flores stopped a stolen Jeep Cherokee. The three occupants of the Jeep were members of an organized car-theft ring. As Flores walked toward the Jeep, one of the thieves hid in the back seat and ambushed the deputy.

Flores was shot four times and collapsed on the street. Neel witnessed the shooting and went to the defense of the deputy. He carried two 9 mm semiautomatics in his truck. Opening fire, he prevented the suspects from continuing to shoot Deputy Flores. Neel shot up one clip and then another. He stated in later testimony before a congressional subcommittee hearing on crime that his greatest fear was that an innocent bystander would get hurt, or that he would be killed by the thieves, and people would think he was one of them.

When their automobile became boxed in, the car thieves attempted to car-jack another vehicle. But Neel drove them away with rapid fire. The suspects finally fled on foot and were captured a few hours later. The fallen deputy recuperated, and Neel was proclaimed by the Harris County Deputy Sheriffs Union to be "Citizen of the Year, 1994."

While writing this book, I have spoken with law enforcement officials, as well as many intended victims of crime who used weapons to protect themselves and others. In addition, I have read trial transcripts, police reports, newspaper accounts, and hundreds of related documents. I have read thousands of pages of research concerning gun violence.

I have tried to be as accurate as possible in reporting the incidents described. All stories are documented and can be obtained through public records.

In the final section of most chapters, I have given the would-be victim a forum, quoting directly from interview sessions. Many speak with great poignancy about the life-threatening experiences they endured. Others state their views on related issues, such as gun control, crime, and police protection.

The stories that follow belong to the victims. It is my hope that sharing them will shed light on a little known subject.

The Best Defense

When a strong man, fully armed, guards his own palace, his goods are in peace.
                    —*Luke 11:21* (NKJV)

If the chief is found breaking in, and he is struck so that he dies, there shall be no guilt in his bloodshed.
                    —*Exodus 22:2* (NKJV)

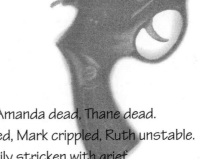

1

Spree Killer

"Brian dead, Tracey dead, Amanda dead, Thane dead.
Reid orphaned, Sue widowed, Mark crippled, Ruth unstable.
Countless friends and family stricken with grief.
Not a bad day's work.

The score is 4 to 0.
Even if they execute me it will still be 4-1."
—From a cell poem of Jerry Hessler

There are two conflicting opinions about Jerry Hessler. A psychologist at his trial told the court, "Mr. Hessler has a severe and long-term mental illness." The man who stopped his murderous spree, Doug Stanton, begged to differ. "He's evil!" Stanton said.

On November 19, 1995, Brian and Tracey Stevens stood in the living room of their house on 356 East Tulane Road in Columbus, Ohio. It was 7:10 P.M., and their friend Ruth Canter was visiting. Tracey held 5-month-old Amanda as 8-year-old Reid sat in the living room watching television. Brian and Tracey worked at Bank One, and Ruth Canter was a former employee of the company.

Canter was expecting her daughter to visit, so she glanced out the living room window. "I see something strange on the porch," she told Brian. He looked outside and saw a five-gallon gas can that had not been there a few minutes before.

Canter and Brian Stevens stepped out to the porch to investigate. From the darkness, Jerry Hessler appeared. Hessler was a former coworker at Bank One who'd been fired a year ago for sexually harassing Tracey Stevens and other female coworkers. He was currently under court order to stay away from Tracey.

Canter and Brian ran for the door. Brian slammed it shut and locked it, shouting a warning to the other family members.

Hessler kicked the flimsy door twice, shattering it. He pushed aside what was left and entered, brandishing a Smith & Wesson 9 mm automatic pistol. Hessler took aim at Brian Stevens and fired once. The bullet hit Stevens in the abdomen, then ricocheted up into the aorta. Stevens dropped to the floor in a puddle of blood.

Ruth Canter rushed to the back of the house, followed by young Reid. She pushed the boy under the kitchen table, then tried to find a place to hide herself.

In the front of the house, the 9 mm erupted again and again. Six shots hit Tracey Stevens. Amanda was struck twice, in the abdomen and the right leg.

Then Hessler went after Canter. He cornered her in a closet and fired three shots through the door. One round tore through her leg—the others missed.

Jerry Hessler bounded out the door, overlooking Reid Stevens who remained hidden under the table.

Ruth Canter dragged herself to a telephone and called 911.

Columbus Police Officer Curt Radabaugh promptly responded. Upon arrival he found a bloody woman standing outside, hysterical, screaming that everyone was dead.

Ambulances quickly arrived and rushed the victims to the hospital. Paramedics desperately tried to save 5-month-old Amanda. Halfway to Children's Hospital, they lost her pulse. The trauma of losing an infant under such conditions was so devastating that the entire ambulance crew had to undergo counseling.

Later that evening, Brian and Tracey also died.

• • •

On the seat beside him, Jerry Hessler had a roster of eight people he intended to kill. Also in the car were a survival kit, extra clothing, four cans of gasoline, eleven boxes of matches, a U.S. passport, and seven hundred dollars in cash.

Hessler drove north to 3157 Indianola Avenue. Mark Campolito, Hessler's former supervisor at Bank One, answered a knock on his door at approximately 8:00 P.M. He saw Jerry Hessler, illuminated by a hundred-watt bulb, pacing back and forth on his porch.

"Hey, Mark," Hessler called out, "I feel awful that I left Bank One on such bad terms."

Campolito was confused. He'd heard that Hessler held a big-time grudge against him. Campolito didn't want to hurt Hessler's feelings, but he also didn't want him hanging around his house. Eventually courtesy won out. He invited Hessler inside.

As soon as Hessler entered, Campolito knew he'd made a mistake. He excused himself and walked to his bedroom to put on his shoes, thinking he might end up in a fistfight. If he had to struggle with Hessler, he wanted his feet to be able to grip the floor. But when Campolito got to the bedroom door, Hessler raised his gun and fired three times. A bullet burned through Campolito's left arm. He twisted away from the shot and dove behind his bed.

"I saw his profile and the gun," Campolito later said.

"He had the damn thing pointed at me, but the next couple of shots whizzed by me. He did nothing to adjust his aim for the second and third shots. I'm convinced he didn't see me turn, or we wouldn't be having this conversation."

Campolito grabbed a loaded .30-.30 rifle from under his bed, chambered a shell, and fired into the ceiling. Hessler fled as Campolito pointed the rifle at the doorway while he called 911. He was quick to warn the dispatcher that Hessler might be hunting down other employees of Bank One.

Campolito was rushed to Ohio State University Medical Center. He would survived, but his injuries required several surgeries, including eighteen pins and two plates that went to reconstruct his shoulder.

Hessler continued north to 233 Franklin Avenue in Worthington.

Sue Griffin was on the telephone with her daughter, Laurie, who lived in Hawaii. When the doorbell rang, she listened as her husband, Thane, answered it. She later testified, "I heard three noises. Laurie said it sounded like gunshots, and I said, 'Nah, it couldn't be.'"

To humor Laurie, Sue laid the telephone down and went to check on her husband of forty-two years. To her horror, she found him bleeding to death near the front door. Later, when the gunman was identified, the only connection Sue Griffin could make with Jerry Hessler was that he'd once had a crush on her daughter. Laurie had never dated him.

Thane Griffin had recently retired from the United Way after thirty-two years of dedicated service. A lifelong champion of the underdog, he'd worked tirelessly to make life better for those who fall through the cracks of society.

At the Columbus Police Department, Lt. David Watkins ordered a statewide alert for officers of any jurisdiction to stop Jerry Hessler for questioning about three homicides (at the time, police had not connected Hessler to Griffin). Hessler was described as 38 years old, approximately six feet tall, two hundred pounds, with short, dark hair and brown eyes. The car he was driving was reported to be a blue 1987 Chevrolet Nova.

Columbus police sergeant Denise Reffitt heard the APB and concluded that she might be able to warn some of Hessler's intended victims. She drove to the house of Jody Hessler, the suspect's brother, and learned the names of several people that Hessler held grudges against. Among the individuals named was a former girlfriend, Judy Stanton.

Sgt. Reffitt knew Hessler and the Stantons well. Years earlier, they all had been active in the Mormon church in Westerville. Now, however, no one seemed to know where Judy Stanton had gone. What Reffitt didn't know was that Judy, her husband, Doug, and their four children had fled the Columbus, Ohio, area to escape from Jerry Hessler.

Intermittently, for fifteen years, Hessler stalked and harassed the Stanton family. Court orders could not restrain him, so the

Stantons moved to Ashland in 1990. They enjoyed four years of peace before Hessler discovered their new address. Now he'd threatened to kill them.

Sgt. Reffitt called Judy's brother, Jeff, and obtained the Stanton's telephone number. She dialed and redialed continuously for several minutes, but couldn't get through. Finally, she persuaded an operator to break in on the call. But before Reffitt could make contact, Judy's brother Jeff reached her.

"Jerry Hessler's on a rampage!" he shouted. "He's killed three people and shot several others. He may be on his way to your house. Get out and go somewhere safe! *Now!*"

As soon as Judy hung up with Jeff, the telephone rang again. Denise Reffitt warned Judy that Hessler might be coming after her. Sgt. Reffitt also said that it was likely that he was wearing a bullet-proof vest. She urged the Stantons to flee and call her when they'd found a secure hiding place.

• • •

Doug Stanton had been preparing for this day for fifteen years.

Jerry Hessler had met Judy Stanton in 1976 at the Church of Jesus Christ of Latter-day Saints in Westerville, Ohio. They dated briefly, but Judy broke off the relationship. Hessler was possessive and demanding, even though at times he seemed devout. He became a missionary in Kentucky, while Judy went to California. They corresponded and even mentioned marriage in some of their letters.

They both returned to Columbus in 1980 and resumed seeing each other. But after a couple of months, Judy broke up with

Hessler for good. A short time later, she began dating Doug Stanton. Also a Mormon, Stanton was attending Ohio State University. When told of their engagement, Hessler confided to Judy that he had a dark side and wanted to hurt Doug.

After Doug and Judy married, they first tried to mollify Hessler. They invited him to dinner, only to have him tell Doug, "I feel like Jesus sitting down to dinner with Judas." Later that evening, Hessler, a National Guardsman, said to Doug, "You know, I've been trained to kill people. I could take you out right now." The newlyweds took the threat seriously and demanded that Hessler stay away from them.

A few weeks later, a campaign of harassment began. Hessler would sit in his car outside their home for hours. At church, he approached the couple and asked probing, intimate questions. Hessler also mailed love letters to Judy, as well as unwanted Christmas packages and birthday cards. Doug became so concerned that he borrowed a shotgun from his father.

In 1985, the Stantons moved to Battle Creek, Michigan, in part to get away from their former friend. They asked relatives and friends not to give Hessler their address. But shortly after they settled in, a package without a return address turned up in the mail. Inside was a letter from Hessler. More packages arrived but were promptly thrown away.

For the first time, Doug began to experience a cold, stark fear, both for himself and his family. He devised safety drills, which he participated in with Judy and their four children. For instance, he would clap his hands and they would drop to the floor and try to find something to hide behind. Had the family not considered

Hessler a clear and present danger, the drills would have seemed bizarre. In fact, a few acquaintances told Doug that he was paranoid, even a control freak. But Doug and Judy had seen the hatred in Hessler's eyes and knew he was dangerous.

Doug bought several weapons, including a Walther PPK .380 automatic and a .45, Model 1911. He sought advice from policemen and Vietnam veterans about how to protect himself and his family. And he spent long hours on the firing range, learning to hit what he aimed at.

In May 1990, Doug and Judy Stanton moved to Ashland, Ohio, about an hour's drive from the Columbus area. They left no forwarding address, canceled magazine subscriptions, and told family and friends not to tell Hessler where they were living.

Jerry Hessler, meanwhile, had drifted from one low-level job to another. Then, in November 1991, he obtained a position at the Bank One complex in Westerville, working in the credit card division as a customer service representative. Several female coworkers, including Tracey Stevens, complained to management about Hessler's unwanted attentions. He was reprimanded on several occasions. Finally, in October 1994, he was fired.

On May 10, 1995, Hessler was committed to Central Ohio Psychiatric Hospital. While at home, he had tried to destroy the interior of his mother's house, kicking holes in the walls and damaging furniture. Against his family's wishes, Hessler was released in July. He was given anti-psychosis medication by a staff psychiatrist, but no controls were put in place to assure he took it.

• • •

At 10:05, Sunday night, November 19, the nightmare that Doug and Judy Stanton had envisioned for so long was about to become reality.

Judy Stanton ran down the stairs screaming, "We've got to leave now! Jerry's on a rampage. He's killed a bunch of people and he's coming here!"

Kira, 8, was in bed. Ben, 11, was playing in his room. Greg, 4, and Amber, 13, were in the living room.

Doug grabbed his two pistols and a .30-.30 deer rifle. On second thought, he decided to leave the rifle behind. It was powerful enough to penetrate a bullet-proof vest, but it might also pierce the walls of the houses across the street. Doug hoped to load his family in his car and be gone before the assassin showed up. If cornered, he would make his stand with the pistols.

Judy herded the children along, each carrying a sleeping bag. They hurried down the stairs, turning off lights as they went.

Outside, Jerry Hessler stood in the driveway. Earlier that day, he'd committed himself to destroying everyone who'd done him wrong. He figured he'd gotten off to a good start.

While driving to Ashland, he'd reloaded the magazine of his 9 mm semiautomatic. Now, he walked toward the back door, holding it in his hand. He was determined to erase the entire Stanton family from the face of the earth. As he'd told friends on many occasions, Judy Stanton should be his wife, and her children should be his.

When he saw the lights click off one at a time, he thought the family was going to bed. And that suited his purpose just fine.

Doug and Judy were pleased at the precision with which the

children remembered their instructions. They'd practiced this drill so many times—now the hours of repetition were paying off. As they reached the kitchen, the phone rang. Doug picked it up and heard Judy's sister on the line.

"Is everything all right?" she asked.

"No, it's not all right," Doug answered. "We'll call you later."

The family huddled behind Doug as he opened the back door. He turned to Judy and said, "Stay in the house for fifteen seconds to give me a chance to make sure everything's clear."

He cocked his .45, making sure the safety was off.

Doug almost fainted when he saw Jerry Hessler coming around the back porch. Hessler wore a trench coat and held a gun in his hand. The odd thought struck Doug that he looked like one of the James-Younger gang in the movie *The Long Riders.*

Stanton darted back into the kitchen and slammed the door shut. He pushed Judy and the kids down on the floor.

"Amber, go down in the basement!" he ordered, momentarily disoriented.

Then he had a second thought. "No!" he shouted. "Stay here. Get down on the floor."

Hessler knocked on the door. "Will you help me?" he asked, sounding sick. "Please!"

"No! Go away!" Without the phone call, Stanton might have relented.

"Please, help me."

"No! Go away."

"Please, Doug. Won't you help me?"

"I'm armed! Go away!"

There was silence. Stanton knew he was coming.

Doug went down on one knee beside the refrigerator. He aimed the .45 at the door and waited.

Hessler wasted no time. He fired three shots at the doorjamb. The yellow flashes that spurted through the darkness were even more frightening than the deafening explosions from the Smith & Wesson. Hessler kicked open the door, sending splinters of wood flying. He stepped into the doorway, silhouetted by the lights of a neighbor's house. Some of the children whimpered, but lay on the floor as they'd been trained. Hessler sprayed bullets into the kitchen, streaks of fire that missed the children by inches.

Doug used the handle of the refrigerator to help him aim. He pulled the trigger and the .45 roared. In the darkness the bullets looked like tracers. The first shots whined high and wide. Doug heard them hitting the door. So he lowered his aim.

Then one of the bullets found its mark, and Hessler staggered backward, clutching his chest. He fell off the porch, and Doug lost track of him for a minute. Then he watched Hessler pull himself to his feet and lurch away to his car.

The car moved slowly away, without headlights.

In the darkness, Doug took a roll call.

"Judy, you okay?"

"Yes."

"Greg, you okay?"

"Yes."

"Kira, you okay?"

"Yes."

"Ben, you okay?"

"Yes."

"Amber, you okay?"

No answer.

Panicking, Doug screamed louder. "Amber, you okay?"

Again there was no answer.

"*Amber, are you okay?*"

"Y-yes, I'm scared."

Relief overwhelmed Doug. "So am I, Punkin," he replied. "So am I."

He grabbed the telephone and called the dispatcher to report the shooting. She told him officers were en route; his call was the fifth one she'd had about the shooting.

Doug and Judy pulled their children together and said a quick prayer. They thanked God they were safe, then prayed for help to arrive quickly.

Doug threw the empty .45 to the floor and yanked the .380 from his pocket. For all he knew, Hessler was crazy enough to return. Stanton believed he'd hit him but didn't know the severity of the wound.

After cocking the gun and clicking the safety off, Doug stood at the door and waited. In the distance, sirens sang and flashing lights came closer.

The telephone rang, startling him. It was the dispatcher. She told him to lay his gun down and walk outside.

When he opened the door, he saw dozens of police cars sitting on his lawn, red lights flashing, headlights on bright. Police officers stood in front of the beams, guns drawn and trained on him. The sight intimidated Doug almost as much as Hessler had.

He raised his hands as high as he could and walked out on the porch.

"Get them hands higher," an officer shouted. "You'll be sorry if you lower them even an inch."

Doug was actually afraid he would fall off the rickety porch and be gunned down by police.

After he was handcuffed and made to kneel behind one of the police cars, Judy and the children were ordered to come out of the house. They, too, were made to raise their hands before being allowed to go to a neighbor's house.

Doug was driven to the police station. His hands were trembling so badly that it was an hour before he could sign the Miranda form. After being questioned for three hours, he was allowed to go home. He was assured that no charges would be filed against him.

At 10:42 P.M., Ashland patrolman Dave Lay spotted a blue 1987 Chevrolet Nova turning onto East Main Street. Its lights were off, but the driver quickly flicked them on. An hour earlier, Lay had received a teletype from the Columbus Police Department describing Hessler and the car he was driving. The message indicated he was wanted for questioning in a triple murder. At the time, Lay knew nothing about the shoot-out at the Stanton home.

The officer called for assistance and was quickly joined by patrolman Scott Reinbolt. Lay then pulled over the Nova and ordered the driver out of the car. Hessler came out with his hands up, then dropped to the ground.

When Lay walked up to handcuff him, Hessler said, "I've been shot."

The officers removed the bullet-proof vest and saw a bruised area and some slight bleeding just above the heart.

"It would be like a mule kicking you," one detective speculated when asked what it felt like to be hit with a .45 caliber bullet while wearing a vest.

Hessler was placed under arrest and transported to Ashland's Samaritan Hospital for minor blunt trauma. He was then released to Ashland police.

Investigating officers at the Stanton house found that Hessler had fired eleven rounds. Stanton had fired seven. Several of Hessler's shots passed over the heads of the children by mere inches. Detectives winced when they dug the bullets out of the walls. Several kitchen utensils such as pots and pans also had bullet holes in them. These were duly confiscated for evidence. Four bullets pierced the wall leading to the basement. They would probably have struck Amber had she hid there as her father had first instructed her to do.

• • •

The Stanton family secluded themselves for three days. On November 22, 1995, Doug and Judy Stanton issued a news release in response to media clamor for access to their story. In part, their statement read: "Our family was able to survive this terrible ordeal thanks to receiving advanced warning from a family member and a friend. There were several other factors that enabled us to survive. Those include: turning off and keeping off all lights in our house when we felt our safety was in jeopardy; owning a firearm for our personal protection and receiving thorough training on how to properly use it; and Divine Intervention."

Jerry Hessler murdered four people and wounded two others. Because one of his victims was an infant, public outcry demanded that he receive the death penalty. His attorneys got nowhere in seeking a plea bargain.

While the Stantons were unwilling to come forward and be interviewed by the media, Hessler called several newspapers to boast about the murders. He showed no remorse—indeed, he seemed proud his deeds.

Hessler's "hit list" was eventually published. It listed the names, home addresses, and telephone numbers of six former coworkers at Bank One. In addition, Thane Griffin and a used-car salesman rounded out the list. Griffin had met Hessler only once, and, try as he might, the car salesman couldn't remember even meeting the killer. Doug and Judy Stanton were not on the list since Hessler already knew where they lived.

The defendant went on trial August 29, 1996, before a jury of twelve men and women at Franklin County Common Pleas Court. Judge David W. Fais presided. All the charges against the defendant would be adjudicated jointly. Hessler was facing four counts of aggravated murder and a multitude of lesser charges. If convicted, he could face the death penalty.

The trial lasted nearly five weeks. Several former supervisors testified that Hessler was not performing up to company standards and that he continually made crude, inappropriate, and unwanted sexual remarks to female employees. He had threatened Brian Stevens on several occasions.

Doug and Judy Stanton recounted for the court fifteen years of living in fear of Jerry Hessler. When Hessler kicked in the door and began firing, Doug testified that the "shots looked like columns of fire as they passed through the dark house."

The evidence against Hessler was overwhelming. He was convicted of four counts of aggravated murder, three counts of attempted aggravated murder, one count of felonious assault, one count of burglary, and one count of shooting a firearm into a dwelling. Each guilty verdict also included weapons-related violations that lengthened the sentences.

In a victim's impact statement to Judge Fais, Doug Stanton wrote, "No amount of words can express what the Stanton family has gone through because of Jerry Hessler over the last sixteen years. All we ask is that we don't have to go through it again. If you don't sentence Jerry Hessler to the most severe penalty available to you, under the law, and Jerry Hessler has any chance of getting out of jail alive, you will in effect be sentencing the Stanton family to death. I ask for the court's mercy on my family as only you can grant. Make sure Jerry Francis Hessler never leaves jail alive. Make him accountable for his crimes. Sentence him to death. For the sake of my family's future I ask, no, I beg you."

Judge Fais sentenced Jerry Hessler to death, plus 121 years and a fine of $205,000.

In December 1996, Columbus police sergeant Denise Reffitt was honored as the state's outstanding peace officer of 1996. The award was presented by the Ohio Prosecuting Attorneys Association. Doug and Judy Stanton attended the ceremony to thank Sgt. Reffitt for her part in helping to save their lives.

In an interview in March 1998, Doug stated that he and his family have suffered dramatically because of Hessler's attack. Doug has difficulty sleeping, has frequent nightmares, and cannot even remember shooting at Hessler. Greg believes he was shot in the eye, apparently because of the yellow streaks he saw as the bullets flashed above his face. He sometimes asks his father not to answer the door because it might be another bad man. Amber has nightmares and is afraid when her parents are not nearby.

The family, however, struggles to survive, helped by their religious faith. Stanton writes, "People are quick to espouse the virtues of gun restrictions. [They say], 'If it saves one life, it will be worth it.' Because the Stanton family had a gun, six lives were saved. Had there been restrictions on gun ownership, the Stantons would be dead. This is a fact, not a hypothetical situation!"

2

High Noon

Travis Dean Neel was procl...
of the Year 1994 by the ...
Texas, Deputy Sherif...
the life of Deputy ...
of Neel, age 64...

"I still want to catch a few more crooks b...
That's what I do best."
—*Harris County Deputy Frank Flores*

"I guess they realized that other people have guns, too, that
guns can fire two ways."
—*Travis Dean Neel*

"Shoot-outs usually last mere seconds," said Travis Dean Neel. "But this one went on and on."

It was January 21, 1994, and high noon near Houston. Traffic was light on Colonial Parkway. The first clear day in weeks made the edges of shadows seem sharp as Neel drove his Mazda pickup truck toward the firing range. He had once loved to shoot targets with his assorted firearms, but open-heart surgery had put him down for months. A brain tumor was also discovered and removed, along with the strength he'd once had. In fact, as he approached Mason Road, his cane lay beside him on the seat, a symbol of all he'd lost during his recent illness.

...imed Citizen
...Harris County,
...s Union for saving
...rank Flores. This photo
...was taken March 1998.

...t today would be different. ...el had just been released from his doctor's care and was looking forward to resuming his old hobby. He figured today just might be the start of the long road back.

Five blocks from his home in Katy, Texas, Neel ducked into a moving gap directly behind a Harris County Sheriff's Department car. In addition to his cane, also on the seat were a Merkel shotgun and two 9 mm semiautomatic pistols, one a Czechoslovakian-manufactured CZ.-75 pistol. Before leaving home, he'd loaded three fifteen-round magazines for the CZ.-75, but he had not inserted one in the gun. Neel, a retired gun shop owner, was familiar with Texas gun laws. Neither the shotgun, which was broken down into three parts and carried in a gun case, nor the pistols were loaded.

At Mason Road near the western end of Harris County, an on-coming vehicle, a white Jeep Cherokee, slowed down for the intersection.

Suddenly, the red lights on the police cruiser began to flash. The police car cut in front of the Jeep, stopping it dead in its tracks.

Must be serious, Neel thought, since law officers usually conduct traffic stops from the rear. As the two vehicles stopped, they faced each other, as if standing nose-to-nose. Neel came to a stop, blocked

by the bottleneck. Vehicles began to pile up behind him. The flashing lights from the police car stained the Cherokee a bloody red.

Neel watched the deputy climb out of his cruiser. He approached
cautiously, with his hand on his gun.

From his elevated pickup truck, Neel could see down into the
Jeep, much better than the deputy who was on foot. He thought
he glimpsed three men—two in the front seats, a third in the rear.

Harris County Deputy Sheriff Frank Flores had been a cop for
twenty-five years. In 1991, he'd been named Officer of the Year by
the Mexican-American Sheriffs Organization. His son, Frank Jr.,
and nephews C. F. Olivera and Ben Blanchard were also deputies.

Earlier that day, Flores had returned to the station to fill out
some reports. While doing the required paperwork, he took off
his bullet-resistant vest and almost forgot to put it back on when
returning to patrol duty. After walking part of the way to his car,
Flores remembered the vest, went back in, and strapped it onto
his body.

"Our sergeant," Flores later explained, "jumps us when we
don't wear the vest, but he wasn't on duty. I decided to go back
and get it anyway."

He had been back on patrol about ten minutes when he spotted the Jeep Cherokee. Moments before, a radio dispatch had
gone out regarding a similar vehicle that had been reported stolen
earlier that day. The description of the two occupants in the front
seat matched those of the suspected car thieves, so he decided to
check it out.

Flores called for backup. But in that rural section of Harris
County, no other units were immediately available.

As he walked up to the car, the deputy ordered the two visible occupants outside. He glanced into the back seat but didn't see anyone else. Placing both men against the back of his cruiser, he began to pat them down.

Neel, a veteran of the Korean War, watched the scene, mildly irritated. This was supposed to be the first day of the rest of his life. Behind his truck, a lane formed to the right, allowing some traffic to crawl by. Neel thought about cutting into it, but the steady flow of cars kept him from backing up to pull into the improvised passing lane.

He was stuck.

Neel turned back to see the deputy still searching the two suspects. Something isn't right, Neel thought. He could have sworn he saw three men in the Jeep.

Seconds later, he saw a movement in the back of the Jeep. Before Neel could shout a warning, a man leaped from the Cherokee. He was dressed in black baggies, a dark shirt, and had a black cap placed at a crooked angle across his head.

The deputy was talking to the two suspects, who were spread-eagled against their vehicle, when he heard a noise behind him. With the instincts of a veteran cop, he wheeled toward the sound of the opening door, his hand on his holstered gun. But before he could square up to face the third suspect, a gunshot blasted into him.

The bullet spun Flores completely around.

Neel watched the deputy seize his own weapon, unsnap the holster, then clear leather. The shooter had ambushed Flores so quickly that Neel was momentarily paralyzed.

Flores, still reeling from the blast to his back, squeezed off a round at his assailant.

Then the street erupted with gunfire.

A small war was being waged right in front of Neel. Flores fired four more shots, but because he was trying to twist away from his attacker and shoot at the same time, his rounds went wide.

The gunman, however, had a clear target. Flores was hit three more times. The sights and sounds are burned indelibly into Neel's mind—the flashes of the muzzle in the shooter's hand, the volley of the guns, and the thump of the bullets hitting the wounded deputy. An errant round missed the officer, showering sparks off the hood of his cruiser.

Flores staggered with each shot, then collapsed onto the pavement. Blood stained his shirt and soaked his arms.

Neel later said, "I knew I couldn't go to my grave, or the spirits, knowing I hadn't done anything to help. At that time, I made up my mind to die with the officer."

He grabbed the 9 mm CZ.-75 pistol that lay beside him on the seat, then placed two fifteen-shot magazines in his pocket. He jammed the remaining one into the butt of the gun, but it wasn't as easy as it had once been. Because his left side was still weak from the surgery on his brain, Neel had difficulty snapping the magazine in place. When he was finally satisfied that he had inserted it correctly, he stepped out of his truck to join the fight.

The scene reminded him of Heartbreak Ridge. He'd served in the army during the Korean conflict, and he had seen death firsthand. As he looked at the officer lying on the road, Neel revisited that terrible scene forty years before. He'd been on the frontlines, in the thickest firefights, but his memory had long ago buried those horrors.

Now the nightmare returned.

Neel moved as quickly as he could into the middle of the street, between the fallen deputy and his assailants. He looked for the two suspects that Flores had been searching and saw them hiding behind the Jeep Cherokee.

The gunman was a few feet away from Neel. He snarled a threat at the former gun dealer, and crouched to face his challenger. Fortunately for Neel, the first shot went wide.

Neel raised his own gun and returned fire.

Click!

He pulled the trigger again.

Click!

Oh God, he thought, I'm dead. Shots were suddenly coming at him from behind the van, and Neel realized that at least one of the other suspects was armed. Behind him, a bullet shattered the windshield of the deputy's cruiser. Neel was exposed and knew he had to return fire quickly, or he would soon be lying next to the deputy.

Inspecting his weapon, Neel realized that, in his excitement, he'd placed the magazine in upside down. He wrestled it out, flipped it over, and lined it up. Because of the weakness in his left hand, he was forced to rest the magazine on his knee and shove it into place.

Now he turned back to the gunman, raised the CZ.-75, and began firing. The semiautomatic weapon suddenly spurted out a volley of gunfire.

The first gunman danced backward, then turned and fled. He

ended up behind the Jeep Cherokee with the other suspects. Now they were all firing at the lone man standing in the street.

At least, Neel thought, they've stopped shooting at the deputy.

On the road, cars gunned their motors and banged into one another in an attempt to flee from the gunfight. One line of traffic was stuck, and the stranded motorists ducked beneath their dashboards. Neel was concerned about the innocent people caught in the deadly trap.

What will happen if I hit an innocent person? he wondered. Or what if the suspects hit someone in one of the cars while they're shooting at me? No one really knew his intentions. No one, that is, except the officer who lay dying on the road. If I'm killed, he asked himself, will people think I was one of the bad guys?

He'd noticed that as soon as he slowed his rate of fire, the suspects responded with a burst of their own. Because of the glare from the sun, he was unable to clearly see the suspects. He decided it was best to keep them pinned down until help arrived. And the best way to do that was with direct volleys of gunfire.

And then his gun froze up. It was empty.

Neel dodged to the back of the police car, hoping to get an angle so that other vehicles would be out of the line of fire. He pushed another magazine into his gun and resumed shooting.

The suspects retreated behind another car.

This allowed Neel the chance to limp back to his truck. He had only one more magazine for the CZ.-75, and besides, he thought, the shotgun would provide more firepower. However, his hands fumbled as he tried to assemble it, and the suspects were shooting at him again.

Suddenly, the three men jumped back into their Cherokee. The engine roared as the driver tried to free it from between the police cruiser and the line of traffic. Metal crunched and glass shattered as the Cherokee rocked back and forth, bouncing against the vehicles that boxed it in. Neel heard the suspects swearing in frustration.

He placed his final magazine into the gun and opened up again. The Jeep was soon riddled with bullet holes. The glare from the sun kept him from getting a clean shot at any of the suspects. And always in the back of his mind was the realization that he might hit an innocent citizen.

The suspects finally decided that the Jeep Cherokee was wedged in too tight to be dislodged. They jumped from the side door and ran west along Mason Road, heading in the direction of the nearby Williamsburg Settlement subdivision.

About fifty feet away, Neel saw a light-colored compact car dodge out of the traffic jam. The driver was trying to weave between several stalled cars, but could not build up sufficient speed.

The suspects ran to the compact.

One gang member reached inside the window in an attempt to open the door. Another circled to the passenger side, then tried to punch his way through the glass window.

The driver's face was silhouetted in the windshield. Neel saw that it was a woman, and she appeared terrified.

He couldn't let the suspects kidnap her. She would be as good as dead in their hands.

Neel cranked off a withering fire now, aiming so that he wouldn't hit the woman in the car.

Off to his right, he heard another gun firing. He glanced to his side and saw another citizen coming to his aid. The new shooter was clean-cut and seemed to be familiar with his weapon. But he didn't have the firepower to match Neel's. The newcomer's .38 revolver sounded like a popgun compared to the high-velocity discharges of Neel's 9 mm.

The suspects had had enough.

They turned on their heels and continued toward the Williamsburg Settlement, a group of upscale homes surrounded by cattle ranches.

A small foreign-made car drove up to a shaken Neel. The driver was a woman holding a baby.

She rolled down her window and asked, "You need another gun?"

"Go call the police," Neel said. "Tell them an officer's down, and they need to get here fast."

As she pulled away, he shouted, "Tell them they're gonna need some real firepower down here—maybe some choppers in the air, too."

During the firefight, dozens of calls had jammed the 911 system of both the Houston Police Department and the Harris County Sheriff's Department. Most callers told dispatchers that an officer was down and backup was needed. Some gave a play-by-play broadcast of the running gun battle.

Neel turned to help the downed officer. He was startled when he saw the wounded man stand up. His hand was drawn like a bloody claw, and his finger still held on to the trigger guard of the gun that dangled from his finger.

"He had holes all over him," Neel later said. "All I could see was holes."

Neel and Robert Grigar, an off-duty Harris County sheriff's deputy, attempted to get the officer to lie down. But the dazed cop mumbled that he was going to "chase" the suspects.

By now, Neel realized that Grigar was the second gunman, the one whose .38 sounded like a cap pistol. After Neel and Grigar guided the officer back to his cruiser, Grigar grabbed the microphone, pressed the button, and said calmly, "An officer has been shot. Get detectives down here. And we need an ambulance. Quick!"

The static on the radio sounded like an A.M. radio in a thunderstorm. A dispatcher's voice cut through the garbled noise. Neel couldn't make out what she was saying. But Grigar could. "We're at the intersection of Colonial and Mason," he informed the dispatcher.

In the distance, Neel heard sirens wailing toward the scene.

• • •

The first officers to arrive were amazed that Frank Flores was still alive. In the early reports, they'd been told that an officer was dead, and that a war was raging on the highway between car-jackers and citizens.

Responding officers expected to find the road littered with dead bodies.

Neel quickly explained what had happened and pointed officers toward the direction the suspects had run. Deputies quickly began sealing off the subdivision. Within a matter of minutes, they had the suspects trapped inside a perimeter of homes. Teams of heavily armed officers began filtering into the upper-middle-class neighborhood.

The deputies asked Neel to go with them so he could identify the shooters if the authorities found them. In an unusual move, they permitted Neel to carry his gun to protect himself.

Paramedics attended to Flores. The deputy, barely lucid, was incensed that he'd been ambushed and shot. He was still demanding that he be allowed to chase after the crooks who attacked him. As the medics placed him on the stretcher, Flores lunged forward, trying to come off the gurney. Several law enforcement people moved over to help hold him down.

Traffic cops arrived to unscramble the logjam and facilitate the flow of traffic. A Life-Flight helicopter appeared in the sky and sank down onto the road. Paramedics rushed Flores to the chopper and flew him to nearby Hermann Hospital.

Tracking dogs arrived, their handlers grim and snappy. The Harris County Sheriff's Department SWAT Team, locked and loaded, followed the dogs. They reasoned that if the suspects would shoot a police officer, they certainly wouldn't hesitate to shoot any citizen who crossed their paths.

The worst-case scenario was that the suspects might take hostages. By now, darkness had fallen and helicopters lit up the neighborhood with floodlights. Their blades battered the night, while residents stood in groups on street corners to watch the deadly game of hide-and-seek.

Neighboring counties had also responded to the shooting of a fellow officer. A Fort Bend County bloodhound picked up a scent and pulled his handler through back yards, vacant lots, and across a small creek. It was like reading a roadmap of where the suspects had fled. They'd plunged down an alley into the neighborhood, then cut behind several houses before running down an unlighted street. Finally, the trail stopped a few blocks away at the back door of 22303 Bucktrout Lane.

Deputies approached the house. An 18-year-old resident, Cyrus Sorab Irani, answered the door.

"Did you see anything unusual?" an officer asked.

"I don't know nothing about nothing," a surly Irani mumbled.

Officers weren't convinced. His jacket matched the one worn by the car thief who shot Flores. They were obviously members of the same gang.

"Can we search your house?"

"No way, man."

The officers moved away from the residence and called detectives. The premises were surrounded while officers waited for a search warrant. It arrived shortly, and Harris County deputies went into the house.

As they entered the utility room, they saw a movement.

A deputy, holding his snarling dog on a tight leash, shouted, "Hey, buddy, you're on the menu if you don't come out . . . *Now!*"

Marcus Stiles crawled from behind a washing machine. His face was slick with sweat, and his clothes were dripping.

He was promptly handcuffed and arrested.

Police also took Irani into custody.

During interrogation, both suspects confessed to being members of a car-theft ring. They had already stolen five vehicles that day.

Stiles stated that he had hidden in the back seat when Flores stopped the Jeep. He told the driver and the passenger to divert the deputy until he could get an opportunity to shoot him.

As the suspect confessed, detectives looked for some sign of remorse. They found none. In fact, Stiles seemed proud of his role as the triggerman.

He was charged with attempted capital murder of a police officer, and, because of his gang membership, five counts of engaging in organized crime.

Irani was charged with hindering the apprehension of a suspect, as well as two counts of engaging in organized crime.

Within a few hours, the two suspects who had ridden with Stiles were rounded up. Even though they were juveniles, Jose Eliud Hernandez and Paul Ontiveros were remanded to Circuit Court to be tried as adults. They were also charged with attempted capital murder of a police officer and engaging in organized crime.

Eventually, a total of eight members of the gang were captured, convicted, and sentenced to prison.

• • •

Frank Flores returned to work three weeks later. He had been hit in the back, the chest, the right shoulder, and the left wrist. His vest had stopped the bullets from penetrating his torso. One round would have pierced Flores' heart if he had not been wearing his armor. Instead, it left an ugly purple bruise that lasted for weeks, even after he was cleared to go back to work. Flores continues to patrol the rural sections of Harris County and always wears his bullet-resistant vest.

Robert. C. Grigar, the off-duty deputy who came to the aid of Flores and Neel, returned to work after having been investigated for firing his weapon.

Travis Dean Neel, the former gun shop owner and veteran of Heartbreak Ridge, was honored as a hero. The Harris County Deputy Sheriffs Union declared him 1994 Citizen of the Year.

The proclamation reads:

"Whereas, at 12:20 pm on Friday, January 21, 1994, Harris County Deputy Sheriff Frank Flores stopped a stolen Jeep Cherokee at the corner of Colonial Parkway and Mason Road which was occupied by three men who had stolen the vehicle and were part of an organized car-theft ring; and

Whereas, one of the thieves, in an effort to avoid arrest, hid in the stolen vehicle while Deputy Frank Flores attempted to put the other two under arrest, then ambushed Deputy Flores and repeatedly shot him in the back, upper chest, left shoulder and right wrist with a .38 caliber pistol with intent to take the deputy's life; and

Whereas, there were no other on-duty police officers in the close proximity to Deputy Frank Flores who could come to his aid in time to save the deputy's life; and

Whereas, Travis Dean Neel, a good citizen and Korean War veteran, armed with his own handgun, saw the incident, came to the aid of Deputy Frank Flores, returned fire at the armed thieves and saved Deputy Flores' life; and

Whereas, as a direct result of the heroic actions of Travis Dean Neel, all of the armed thieves were arrested, charged with attempted capital murder of a peace officer and other offenses, and will be brought to justice;

NOW THEREFORE, BE IT PROCLAIMED, on this first day of
February 1994, that TRAVIS DEAN NEEL, is hereby
declared by the members of the Harris County Deputy Sheriffs
Union to be Citizen of the Year, 1994.

Almost exactly a year later, Travis Dean Neel flew to Washington, D.C., to appear before the House Judiciary Subcommittee on Crime and Criminal Justice. The proceedings were televised, and many citizens who had used firearms for self-defense appeared before that committee.

"I want to tell you a story," Neel said, "so that you can answer a question many people ask, about why a citizen might need what they call a 'large-capacity magazine.' When you've heard my story, you might think the large-capacity magazines I had were not large enough."

As he related his experience, members of the committee sat in stunned silence.

"For the past fourteen months," he continued, "I have spent all my waking hours pondering my experience. I've come to these conclusions: First, having those firearms—and those magazines—in the car that day saved my life and that of Deputy Flores. Those who want to ban guns and the magazines that go with them tell you that only a criminal needs access to such large-capacity magazines. But at the scene of that shootout, it was the good people—the deputy and I—who had large-capacity magazines.

"I fired thirty-nine shots that day. The criminal, the would-be assassin, had a six-shot revolver. And a survey of criminals in the county jail afterward found that 85 percent of the armed convicts in custody preferred revolvers or shotguns for their crimes.

"Second, the criminals who attacked us didn't follow the laws governing the carrying of firearms. If they would obey any law, they would not have tried to kill the deputy; they would not be in jail today. They ignored the laws then, and all too many like them will ignore the laws tomorrow.

"[Third], far from being a threat to law enforcement and the general public—I, with my pistols and my fifteen-round magazines—was an asset that day. But if the gun and magazine ban had been in effect a few years earlier, things might have turned out differently. I and other law-abiding citizens will continue to be an asset tomorrow, and I hope the Committee and the Congress will recognize that by repealing the ban [on assault weapons and large-capacity magazines]."

On February 28, 1995, Neel also appeared before the Texas Senate to testify in favor of a right-to-carry law. Due in part to his testimony, the Senate passed the concealed-weapons permit bill that allows law-abiding citizens the right to carry concealed weapons if they meet certain minimal standards.

On March 21, 1995, Neel testified before the Texas House of Representatives, which also passed the law. It was later signed into law by Governor George W. Bush.

In a recent interview, Neel went into even greater detail about the events of that day. His account is remarkable in several aspects. But the fact that he was handicapped from surviving two major surgeries, and almost completely unable to use his left side, was heroic.

"I was accepting my fate, and really, when I started, I didn't even expect to get a shot off. But I was hoping to get a shot off and hit somebody. I thought if I could hit somebody, hit their car, or something, do something to mark these people, that someone else would pick them up later. That was the best I thought I could hope for.

"I thought I would be found lying in the street here with these guns, and police detectives were going to ask themselves or each other, 'What was he doing here?'

"I threw my cane away in the street in order to perform this. I had trouble loading my pistol and to load it I finally pulled my foot up over my knee, across my knee, and stood on one leg. Standing on the sole of my boot, I loaded my gun. This gun had adjustable sights, and in doing that, I knocked the sight out of alignment. But I did get the gun loaded. I had no control of my left hand.

"In the beginning when I was shooting at them, I was just missing. But one thing I did, you see, I was a lieutenant in the infantry for eight years, and one of the things I taught was how to lay down a base of fire. And make it so hot for the other fellow that he can't shoot back. I would shoot two or three shots at one guy, then three or four at another, and then swing back around. They never caught on to what I was doing. They took shelter, and I stayed in the open, in the middle of the street, and just turned and turned and turned. I followed them as they changed position and wouldn't let them gain an advantage on me. They kept trying to close in, but I wouldn't let them. I would meet them halfway, so to speak, and I would shoot a burst or two at them until they would stop and turn around and run back. Being in the open, I had complete eye coverage of everything that was going on. But if I'd hidden behind the car, they could have charged me, and I would have never known they were coming.

"I knew I was going to run out of ammo, so I began back-pedaling to reach my truck to get more magazines. About that time, my pistol locked back, finishing the third magazine. I knew where the other pistol and magazines were, and I got them very quickly. I come back with it, and when they saw I had that they turned and bolted.

"Just at that moment a woman with a baby broke out of the traffic line and drove right up to me. 'I've got a gun,' she said. 'Can I help?'

"If it hadn't been for her words at exactly that moment, I would have killed one of them [the gunmen]. I was lined up to shoot him in the back. But I lowered the gun to find out where this voice was coming from, and I looked down and a small car was right beside me. I'm six-foot-one and I'm looking down into the car and saw that baby there. I said, 'You can help by getting to a telephone. Tell them an officer is down, and we need more help.' You see, I didn't know how many people had been wounded in the crossfire."

By coming to the aid of Harris County Deputy Frank Flores, Travis Neel became a Texas legend. Now, four years later, he still travels the same road to the firing range. His strength is returning, and even with all the honors he's received, Neel remains a modest man.

3

The Great Mississippi Bank Robbery

"It's just like these Grenada boys to bring a two-door sedan to a four-man bank robbery."
—Unidentified Mississippi State Trooper

The invasion was in full swing. It was a good plan, thought Jerome McCuiston, 19, of Grenada, Mississippi. Maybe a great one. At nine o'clock that Friday morning of May 10, 1996, he sat behind the wheel of a 1985 blue Monte Carlo two-door sedan. He'd stolen it Wednesday night from a parking lot in Memphis. He and his partner, Genard Ratcliff, 17, were parked just off Cox Road in a thicket of lush old trees. Below them lay the town of Potts Camp.

McCuiston reached for Ratcliff's roach, drew a hit, then passed it back. He swatted another mosquito—the windows of the stolen car wouldn't go all the way up. That could be a flaw in the plan, McCuiston thought. But he soon shrugged it off. He felt confident that within a couple of hours they'd all be wealthy men, and no lawman's hot breath would be scorching his neck.

Too bad he couldn't take a lot of credit for the plan. Thirty-two-year-old Glenn Tables was the mastermind. Tables was one of the smartest men McCuiston had ever met. He'd even done hard time. During his recent incarceration, he'd figured out how to get filthy rich—quick. He'd chosen his team, brought them together, and over a three-day period they'd hammered out a strategy.

In addition to McCuiston and Ratcliff, Tables had recruited James Boclear, 17. Tables had insisted that the younger men memorize their assignments. If they all knew every phase of the plan, nothing could go wrong.

Tables had patience, and McCuiston viewed him as a sort of prophet, a man with vision. Like his vision of the forty thousand dollars sitting in the bank of that hick town.

They were about to blow through Potts Camp like a fast-moving train. And when the smoke cleared, the women would be quaking with shell shock, and the men crapping in their boots. Jerome McCuiston, meanwhile, would be back in Grenada, laid back and riffling through stacks of folding money.

A gray pickup swung off the highway and nestled up close behind the car. A motorcycle was tied down in the bed, one of the wrinkles that placed this plan above the average and dumped it squarely into the genius category. Tables and Boclear got out of the pickup, walked over to the Monte Carlo and climbed in. McCuiston started the engine, pulled onto Cox Road and headed south.

• • •

Potts Camp lies southeast of Memphis, a forty-minute drive on Highway 78. The road flattens out after reaching the town of Southaven, running past fields where hay lies rolled in huge bundles and cattle and horses appear as tiny dots along the skyline.

The town has about five hundred citizens, but you wonder where they live when you finally come to South Center Street, the town's main drag. There's no Wal-Mart or McDonald's, but it does have a tiny post office, a convenience store, and a couple of gas stations. The main attraction is Taylor's Cafe, a small diner that sits directly across the street from the Potts Camp bank.

At about 9:40 A.M., Don Carver, a local Methodist minister, was driving down South Center Street when he saw an unfamiliar vehicle. It was a blue Monte Carlo, with four occupants, creeping into town from the direction of adjacent Benton County. Aware of a rash of recent burglaries in the community, he jotted down the tag number. Carver also noted that the car pulled over and stopped in front of the bank.

In his office behind the cashier section, 44-year-old Rodney Whaley, vice president and bank manager, put down the telephone and picked up a folder. He'd grown up in Marshall County and had received a degree in business administration at the University of Mississippi in nearby Oxford.

Whaley was a highly respected civic leader. Throughout his fourteen years of managing the branch office for the Bank of Holly Springs, he had made time to contribute to every community cause that could make life better for the people of his county.

His hobbies were target-shooting and hunting, and he'd begun collecting handguns a few years back. In fact, he kept a loaded .357 Magnum in a drawer of the very desk where he was sitting.

At approximately 9:45 A.M., the glass door in the lobby crashed open, and three men burst into the bank. They all wore dark clothing, caps, and stockings to cover their faces.

Whaley, busy doing paperwork, didn't even notice the activity.

Before the tellers could press the panic buttons under their money drawers, two of the men cranked off staccato bursts of gunfire from their semiautomatic pistols.

Rodney Whaley and daughter, Amanda Whaley Shaw. Both were working at the Potts Camp bank the morning of May 10, 1996, when three masked robbers armed with semiautomatic weapons stormed the bank.

"*Get down!*" they screamed in unison, as if they'd practiced giving these orders.

It took a second before the tellers realized what was happening. Then they hit the floor.

"*Get down! Stay down!*"

Amanda Whaley, Rodney's 19-year-old daughter and the operator of teller station number four, dropped to the floor as ordered. On the way down, she managed to brush her alarm button, activating the system monitored by the Marshall County Sheriff's Department. That button also triggered the security cameras.

It had been a slow morning, and Amanda had been reading a novel she kept hidden in the top drawer. As the masked men rushed toward her, Amanda thought of her friends at the University of Mississippi, where she was a sophomore. Then she instinctively crawled into the small space beneath her teller window, keeping her face turned away from the action.

One of the robbers charged through the swinging door that separated the tellers from the waiting room. He pointed his gun at the face of Barbara Pipkin, who had been manning the cash drawer at teller station number one.

"Gimme your money!" he shouted. "Or I'll blow your head off."

Smoke from the gunfire had curled up toward the ceiling.

Pipkin's ears rang as the gunman repeated his command, "Gimme all the money!"

His arm was jerking, and it frightened her. He could accidentally shoot her if he didn't calm down. Pipkin tried to remain calm as she watched him take the money from her cash drawer and stuff it into a plastic bag.

Across the street at the post office, a clerk had seen the men enter the bank with guns drawn. She promptly dialed 911. And at Taylor's Cafe, customers sought cover when they heard the first gunshots.

Back in the office, Rodney Whaley had flinched at the sound of gunfire. A sickening thought struck him: Amanda was out front in the middle of danger.

He looked up at the closed-circuit monitor on his desk. On the screen, a time-lapse VCR snapped a picture every three seconds.

Whaley heard the man at the cashier's station shouting, "Gimme your money! Gimme your money! Gimme your money!"

Through the monitor, Whaley saw that the gunman was having trouble opening one of the cash drawers. Pipkin, who was lying on the floor beneath her station, calmly reached up and tapped the release key. The drawer popped open, and the robber scooped out a bundle of bills.

When the gunman looked up, he must have seen the camera perched above Whaley's office. He stopped grabbing money, turned, and pointed his gun at it.

A blast jarred the door to Whaley's office. The gunman fired twice more at the camera.

My God, this guy's got a hawg, Whaley thought. His hand moved a little faster as he opened the drawer and pulled out his own Magnum.

Amanda pressed deeper into the foot space below her window. When she heard the three shots, she assumed the tellers were being executed one by one. Being teller number four, her turn would be next. Her face was slick with sweat, and she began to hyperventilate.

The robber with the big gun began to skulk toward Rodney Whaley's office.

Whaley eased out of his chair to meet him, holding his revolver in his right hand. He inched to the wall, trying to remain as close to it as possible, while he waited for the robber to try to gun him down.

"When he came through the door," Whaley recalled, "the first thing I saw was his pistol. He had a Ruger SP 101 .357 Magnum with a stainless-steel finish and a six-inch barrel. I can remember seeing a hand holding the gun, but that wasn't as clear as the fact that it was a real pistol. And then he started making little sweeping motions, as if feeling around for a target. Then I realized he was bearing down on me and was probably going to fire.

"His body was just barely through the door when he started swinging around. I had a split second, and I fired three times as quick as I could pull the trigger. The first bullet went through the door facing, which shows you how tight against the wall I was. It went into his right side. The second one went through his right bicep. The impact sort of jerked him up in the air and backward. My third shot went through the inside of his left thigh and out the other side. I was shooting 125 grain hollow points."

As the sound of Whaley's shots reverberated throughout the room, the two armed men in the lobby turned and fled through the entrance door.

Whaley stood in his office door, not quite believing the scene that was unfolding. The robber he'd shot scrambled away, trailing blood across the floor. The tellers still lay beneath their stations, their eyes wide, their faces shell shocked. Whaley glanced at Amanda and saw that she was unhurt.

In the lobby, two customers had dropped to the floor as soon as the robbers entered the bank. Now they lay cringing in terror.

The wounded gunman stumbled past the tellers and on out to the lobby. He was gasping heavily, but still managed to swear under his breath. As he struggled to the door, he dropped his revolver. Then he clambered to his feet and lurched into the street.

Someone yelled, "They're gone!"

When Amanda looked up, she expected to see dead bodies all over the floor. Instead, her father was moving cautiously out into the lobby. In his right hand was a smoking pistol. He was shaking, his face was ashen, and he murmured, "My God. What just happened here?"

"Was anyone shot?" Amanda asked. A catch in her throat made her voice squeak.

She was told that her father had shot one of the robbers.

A customer was on the verge of hysteria. Mumbling incoherently, her hands trembled while she sobbed.

Amanda looked around again, unable to believe that everyone was safe. Breathing a sigh of relief, she took a cup of water to the shaken customer and gently led her to the lounge to await the paramedics.

When he was certain all the robbers were gone, Whaley took a quick head count. Then he locked the doors to await the police.

• • •

In Holly Springs, the Marshall County Sheriff's Department switchboards were lit up like a Christmas tree and the phones were ringing off the hooks.

Sheriff Kenny Dickerson was already calling the shots. At the first alarm, he'd sent every available deputy racing toward the bank. Then he notified other agencies, including nearby DeSoto County. They promised to put their only chopper in the air within minutes. It would patrol as far south as Benton County, looking for the getaway car.

For the robbers, the plan that had looked so good was continuing to slide downhill. Once outside, Ratcliff and Boclear sprinted for the Monte Carlo. The wounded Tables lurched and wobbled, leaving a splotch of blood at every step.

The two robbers, both uninjured, fought each other as they tried to simultaneously climb into the sedan through the half-drawn windows. McCuiston, the driver, screamed for them to open the door. But in their panic they merely clawed at the windows and pushed each other harder.

Whaley, viewing the scene from his office, figured that the doors must have jammed. The wounded man somehow reached the car and managed to open a door and crawl in. Blood dripped from the handle as it slammed shut.

In their frenzy, the other two gunmen never got inside the car. The driver impatiently gunned the engine, and the muffler belched smoke.

Whaley raised his gun and fired. Glass showered back into the office, like a backdraft. As the gunshot resounded, the Monte Carlo sped away, leaving a trail of exhaust fumes and two desperate robbers. They were both knocked back from the car, landing in the street. Whaley watched as they bounded to their feet and bolted for a stand of trees north of town.

But one gunman stopped, then spun around to face the bank. Whaley watched as the gun came up and pointed at him—then he saw a yellow flame spurt from the barrel.

Whaley fired again through the window. As the robbers lurched away, Whaley put his smoking gun on his desk and waited.

Sheriff Dickerson arrived within ten minutes. Deputies and paramedics quickly followed, as well as civilians carrying shotguns and rifles. The sheriff organized the men into a makeshift posse and sent them out to search the woods where the fugitives had last been sighted.

"The staging area that the robbers used was about a mile from the bank," Whaley later explained. "After the robbery, Glenn Tables and McCuiston went back there and switched vehicles. They got out of the stolen car and into Tables's pickup. We discovered later they were going to Grenada, Mississippi.

"The other two guys, had they proceeded according to their plan, would have gotten on the motorcycle and driven away. But they had to stay hidden and sneak through the bushes. And they weren't real sure of their surroundings. By that time the search had been put into motion. People were driving around looking for them.

"Two young boys saw them trying to get on the motorcycle. They hollered, and the robbers fled again."

The haul from the cashier's window was thirty-eight hundred dollars. While on the run, Ratcliff and Boclear hid their loot under some garbage at a picnic area. The money was later recovered, along with the handguns.

By now Tables and McCuiston were roaring toward Grenada. As Tables groaned in pain, McCuiston thought back on their plan. What the hell had happened in that bank? Tables, his hero, had said the place was a pushover. McCuiston wanted to ask him what had gone wrong, but couldn't quite bring himself to question his idol. Tables held his hands over his side, trying to stanch the blood that was spilling out. Coughing and sputtering, he begged McCuiston to take him to a hospital.

In less than an hour, McCuiston had made the eighty miles to Grenada and dumped Tables at the emergency room of the county hospital. It was a remarkable piece of driving, considering that north Mississippi was overrun with law enforcement people.

Back in Potts Camp, the search for the other two robbers had tightened around the staging area. By now, Marshall County deputies were joined by officers from the Mississippi Highway Patrol, the Game and Fish Commission, and deputies from three contiguous counties. The FBI office in Memphis had dispatched special agents, who were due to arrive shortly.

Dickerson later gave credit to his colleagues. He said, "We really appreciate the support from all the agencies who helped us. The detail stood close together. It was that organization that led us to the capture of the two suspects."

Dozens of civilian volunteers were also out looking. They were first briefed about what to do if they made contact with the suspects: capture them, if possible, and fire only if fired upon. Each volunteer knew he would be held accountable if a suspect was shot while posing less than a clear and compelling danger.

Many of the volunteers were placed as sentinels on bridges, highways, and carports. Sheriff Dickerson also dispatched a mixed group of deputies and volunteers to guard the Mary Reid School, which was near the robber's staging area. Their assignment was to ensure the safety of the schoolchildren and the employees who worked there.

At approximately five o'clock that afternoon, James Carl Pipkin, a volunteer, was feeling edgy. He'd been watching a spot of ground near the forest area into which the fugitives had first fled. Pipkin had been hearing faint noises for a couple of minutes, but he knew that a tense man can sometimes hear imaginary sounds. Then he heard a distinct rustling in the brush. He trained his rifle on the noise. The two robbers appeared.

"Get down on the ground!" Pipkin ordered.

By now, the fight was out of them. They fell to their knees, hands above their heads. Pipkin radioed in a report of the apprehension to the dispatcher in Holly Springs.

While awaiting the arrival of sheriff's department personnel, Pipkin stepped over to the subdued robbers.

"The only thing keeping you alive," he said, "is that you didn't hurt my wife."

When one of the captives looked at him quizzically, Pipkin said, "My wife, Barbara, was one of the tellers. If you'd hurt her, you'd be a dead man now."

Law enforcement authorities soon received word that Glenn Tables had checked into the Grenada City Hospital. His wounds were so severe that he would have died had he waited another half hour for treatment. He was airlifted to the trauma unit of the Memphis Regional Medical Center. Mississippi officials arrived a few hours later. Tables was duly read his rights and placed under arrest. A guard station was set up outside his room until he recovered, at which time he was returned to Marshall County.

Jerome McCuiston was arrested two days later near his home in Grenada, still wondering what had gone wrong.

All the robbers were incarcerated at the Marshall County Jail. Each man's bail was set at $100,000.

• • •

In a recent interview, Rodney Whaley recounted his feelings about the day he was forced to shoot a man.

"I was scared. When Sheriff Dickerson got to the bank—of course, he'd already heard the radio reports and knew about what had happened—I said, 'Son, am I in trouble?' He said, 'Not with me, you're not.' Of course, I was glad to hear that because you can't help but wonder what our crazy laws might do to someone.

"By noon that day, the FBI people showed up, and I asked, 'Do y'all think I'm in trouble?' and they said, 'Nope. If that wasn't justified, I don't know what is.'

"By Monday morning the county prosecutor had called and said, 'Don't worry about being in trouble. You did what you had to do. You won't be prosecuted.' That was extremely refreshing. It took a tremendous load off my mind.

"I had an opportunity to talk to Boclear and Ratcliff. They said they had inside information; they knew I kept a pistol in the bank. They said, 'We knew the dude in the bank had a gun, and Glenn's plan was to get in there and stop him before he could get it.'

"It's by the grace of the good Lord that I was even able to think about getting my gun. The whole incident all happened in just a few seconds.

"All of the law enforcement personnel were very supportive. We found it real refreshing that they were of that frame of mind. We expected to be chastised for having guns and shooting back, considering the liberal society we live in. But that wasn't the case down here.

"Another ironic note was that I had about a dozen different law enforcement people come by and tell me if I'd used a particular cartridge, Tables wouldn't have got out the door. Now I've got a whole desk drawer full of cartridges of various sizes and weights and grains and powders that they gave me."

Amanda Whaley Shaw continues her studies at Ole Miss, majoring in journalism. She recently wrote of her feelings about that day: "I dreamt about the experience many nights afterward and it always nauseated me. I lost weight, and I lost sleep. I'm just thankful I didn't lose my mind. . . . I still wonder today if we would have all been killed if my dad hadn't had a gun.

"[For months after the robbery], at night, lying in bed, I heard every tiny noise. I got to the point where I wanted to be the first in my house to fall asleep, so that any noise I heard could be credited to the others.

"We went back to work on Monday and managed to open for business. The fact that we [the tellers and others who worked in the bank] were all good friends made it easier. A funny thing that we all discovered was that although we found it hard to talk to others about the experience, we could easily discuss it with each other.

"I always thought I wanted to forget it, but I don't. It's not even possible. Although exact details fade, the impact is still there. It occasionally reminds me that I have so much to live for. Life is short and can be shorter, so my memories encourage me to live each day to the fullest."

● ● ●

By October 1996, each defendant had cut a deal with the district attorney's office.

Glenn Tables was sentenced to ten years without parole. Al Genard Ratcliff received eight years, while Boclear and McCuiston each were given seven-year sentences.

4

A Victim in Paradise

"I used to love to open the windows and doors and feel the Gulf breezes flowing through my house. I got pleasure from watching sailboats and yachts pass by in the canal behind my home. Now I sit in a closed-up room. I'm even afraid to answer the door."
—Sammie Foust

Six-twenty-three A.M.

Sammie Foust will never forget the time.

Her home sat near a canal in an upper-middle-class neighborhood in Cape Coral, Florida. Multicolored hibiscus created a rainbow of colors on the lawns. Orange and lemon trees grew in front of the homes, and palm trees waved in the breeze. Crime was so rare that many neighbors left their doors and windows unlocked.

Foust had spent the night of May 9, 1996, cleaning. The master bedroom was a wreck. The bed was overloaded with bags of clothing Foust intended to give away. Old purses, pillows, and boxes of odds and ends also rested on the bed.

While cleaning out a chest of drawers, she'd turned up a long forgotten gift—a .25 caliber semiautomatic handgun. Years before, a friend had insisted she take it and keep it for protection. In the drawer beside it were four soft-nosed bullets. Curious, Foust pulled out the magazine, then pushed the shells into it. It was harder than she'd imagined. Once the magazine was filled, she jammed it back into the butt of the gun and pulled back the lever. She heard the round snap into the chamber. Then she placed the gun beside a stack of pillows near the headboard.

A gray light from the coming day filtered in through the shades. The 49-year-old divorcée picked up the remote control and turned on the television set. The local anchorwoman dutifully announced the time and weather forecast.

Deciding to take a break and watch a few minutes of the local news, she walked to the bed and leaned back on the pillows. Because it was piled high, there was barely enough room for her to sit. She was wearing a duster, a gown of sorts, with large pockets on either side.

In the dining room, she heard the chains rattle, a familiar noise caused by her cat bumping the vertical blinds. Moments earlier, she'd opened the sliding glass door to let the cat out, so she assumed it was coming back inside.

Looking into the dining room, she was startled to see someone in her house. She quickly concluded it was a man—he wore a jacket, a stocking over his head, and gloves on his hands. At a glance, she estimated that he was over six feet tall and weighed more than two hundred pounds. Foust tipped the scales at slightly more than a hundred.

This is not real, she thought. Who is this? Caught completely off guard, Foust was frozen.

The man wasted no time. He rushed into the bedroom and

lunged at her. She was so surprised she didn't even have time to steel herself. He placed his left hand over her mouth, then pushed her head back into the pillows. A box-cutter knife was in his hand. Foust's eyes widened when she felt the blade prick her throat. The man slashed downward.

It was like an out-of-body experience. Foust knew he'd cut her, but she didn't feel it. The assailant pressed against her body, brandishing the blade in her face.

"Is anybody else here?" he demanded.

Foust couldn't answer because his hand was clamped tightly on her mouth. She tried to shake her head, but his grip was too tight.

"Anybody else here, bitch?"

She finally squeezed out a muffled sound.

"Uh-uh."

The assailant took his hand off her mouth.

As Foust quivered on the bed, he placed the blade between her eyes. Then he brought it down in a slashing motion. It gashed her cheek, biting like a weasel.

Her assailant placed the tip of the blade against her forehead, then slid it down to rest on her nose. Her eyes crossed as she tried to watch the blade.

Now free to talk, Foust said, "Please don't do this. God knows, I'll give you what you want! Plea-ea-se don't do this."

"Shut up, bitch!"

"Please . . ."

"Gimme your money!"

The assailant got up and backed away, giving Foust the opportunity to reach for her purse. She passed it over, and he dumped the contents out on the bed. Keys, makeup, then four hundred dollars in bills spilled out. He fumbled for the money, and Foust realized he wasn't wearing gloves after all. He wore a man's sock on each hand.

Her attacker scooped the money off the bed and thrust it into his pocket. Then he moved back over to Foust. He raised his fist and cracked her on the jaw. Foust saw bursts of light dance somewhere out in front of her eyes as her attacker punched her again and again.

"I want your *big* money!" he said.

"I don't have any more."

He sliced her cheek again.

"Please stop!" Foust begged.

"I want more money."

"There *is* no more money," Foust whimpered. She still harbored a faint hope that he would take everything he could carry and leave.

The man was breathing heavily. Every time he exhaled, the stocking mask blew up like a balloon.

"Give me your jewelry."

"It's over there." Foust pointed to a credenza, or console, across the room. The television set was on it, and on the top of the television was her jewelry box.

Foust lay on the side of the bed, her head still bunched against the pillows. Her legs dangled off the edge of the bed, but her feet didn't touch the floor.

Then she noticed the .25. When her friend had given it to her, her father had told her it was too small. "Get a bigger gun," he said. "Wounded dogs will bite you. Dead dogs don't bite."

Foust was about to learn the truth of that adage.

The gun lay within inches of her right arm, in plain view. She silently prayed to God that her attacker would not see it.

He grabbed the jewelry box and emptied it on the bed. Scooping a few rings into his pocket, he moved back to Foust. She felt another blow against her already swollen face. As she cringed, her attacker punched her again.

Finally he leaned down and laid the tip of the knife on her forehead.

"You bitch! This stuff's nothing but shit! Give me your *real* diamonds."

He paused, huffing and blowing from his effort.

"You know I'm gonna kill you!" he hissed. "So you might as well give it up. Die easy or die hard, bitch!"

It was then that Foust decided to go for the gun. She had to find an opportunity.

The man jerked her to her feet and dragged her across the room.

"Give me your real stuff!" he demanded again.

"I can't," Foust cried. "I'm too nervous. But there's another box over there."

She pointed at a second box on the credenza. It contained only costume jewelry, Foust knew. But she needed space between them so she could get her hand on the gun.

Her attacker flung her back onto the bed. Then he turned and stepped toward the other box.

Foust had never fired a gun. She debated whether to even pick it up. Will it fire if I pull the trigger? she wondered. Even in this deadly predicament, she still had the composure to think her decision through.

Pick up the gun! something told her. *If you don't do it now, you're dead.*

Foust reached down and grasped the handle. She stood up. The man was approximately six feet away. Knowing she was no marksman, Foust aimed for the largest area of his body, the center of his torso.

Then she pulled the trigger.

She half expected her assailant to fly backward, crash against the credenza, and crumple dead on the floor. That's how it happened in countless movies and television shows.

It didn't work quite that way.

The gunshot sounded no louder than a cap pistol. There was no explosion, no bang, no percussion. She wondered if the gun had even fired.

The man turned and looked at her. He didn't bounce backward. She didn't see a hole in his shirt. And she didn't see any blood.

Without warning, he charged across the room. As he body-slammed her down on the bed, Foust managed to fire again, this time holding the .25 against his body.

Then his fist hit her square in the face. She literally heard her nose implode back into her skull.

Dear God, she prayed, *don't let me pass out. Dear God, please let me hold on to this gun.*

Her attacker yanked her off the bed, and they stood breast-to-breast, fighting for the weapon. He gripped her wrist, wrenching at the .25. With his other hand, he slammed her face with jackhammer blows.

Foust clenched her fingers so tightly around the handle that she felt blood vessels bursting in her hand.

As they fought, she decided to wait until she had a clear shot before firing again. She was afraid she would shoot herself, or maybe catch a ricochet. And she didn't have any cartridges to waste.

Finally, her chance came. After a particularly vicious flurry of blows, the attacker drew back his arm as if to put his shoulder into a knockout punch. Foust leaned away and twisted until the .25 pointed at his stomach. Then she squeezed the trigger.

Again there was no reaction from her attacker.

He tore her from the bedroom into the dining room, still beating her. She was now able to duck away from a few of his blows. But many more found their mark. Some landed on the neck, some on the back, and some pummeled the back of her head.

In the dining room, Foust pointed the gun toward his abdomen and fired her last bullet. She couldn't believe he was carrying four rounds inside his body and still punching her with the force of a heavyweight fighter.

"Bitch!" he whispered. "Now I'm gonna take that gun and blow your brains out!"

Foust couldn't let on that the gun was empty. She knew if he took it away, he would beat her to death with it. So she squeezed even tighter.

"We struggled into the dining room," Foust recalled. "We fought all over the dining room, from wall to wall. He knocked me into furniture. He beat on me continually. He finally got me in a bent-over position,where he could pound the back of my head at will."

They ended up back near the master bedroom door.

Foust felt a warm liquid dripping on her feet. Maybe her attacker was bleeding to death. She looked down, hoping to see a red stream.

But it wasn't red. It looked more like water.

The man was urinating on her.

He mustered one final, savage blow to the back of her head, and she went down, slamming her face into the tiles. Her head exploded, and she lay exhausted beneath her attacker.

"He was breathing super hard," Foust said later. "But he was still beating at my head and still held my wrist."

She could fight no more. She thought for an instant of her once-beautiful house, then breathed a silent prayer for her loved ones.

She began to pray out loud.

"Our Father in heaven, hallowed be Thy name. . . ."

A blow to the face nearly broke her neck.

"Forgive us our sins as we forgive others. . . ."

The weight of the man held her fast against the tile. She couldn't squeeze out from under him.

"Deliver us from evil . . ."

Foust later recalled her attacker's last moments.

"I said, Lord, I can't fight anymore. I've lost my fight. Forgive me of my sins, and forgive this man for what he's done. At the moment I said that out loud, I felt him release his last breath."

Now his weight became even heavier. She tried to roll from under him. But they were stuck in the doorway, and the man was wedged tightly on top of her.

It took her ten minutes to wriggle free. Finally she stood, dazed and battered. She wandered about the dining room for a moment, then decided to go to a neighbor's house for help.

She walked out through the same sliding glass door her attacker had entered an eternity ago.

Foust didn't realize that she looked like the victim in a slasher movie. Blood pumped in spurts from her nose, and her cheekbones bulged grotesquely. A crimson gash circled her throat. Her lips were swollen like balloons ready to burst.

She walked into the yard, past the hibiscus and fruit trees, and headed next door. For those neighbors who saw her limping toward their houses, it must have seemed impossible that this could be Sammie Foust.

She remembers that the neighbors in the first house refused to admit her.

She went to another house and knocked on the door. No one answered. As she moved away across the yard, she heard a voice shout, "Get off my lawn. You're bleeding on my grass."

Foust looked down and saw blood. Must be his blood, she thought.

She moved to the next house where a neighbor called the police.

● ● ●

A patrolman from the Cape Coral Police Department arrived almost immediately. Within minutes, dozens of police officers, paramedics, and firefighters had converged outside the house. They found Foust standing in a driveway.

She told an officer that a masked man had broken into her house. "I killed him!" she exclaimed.

Police circled her residence but were reluctant to enter. Other assailants could be holed up inside. So they knelt, guns drawn, and waited for the canine unit.

The police asked Foust to go to an ambulance for treatment, but she refused. She was led to a police car where she told an investigator what had happened.

Then, as an afterthought, she took the little pistol out of her duster pocket.

"Would you like to have this?" she asked.

The investigator shouted to a patrolman across the street, "She's got the weapon!" Gloves and a plastic bag were rushed to him from another car.

Foust recalled, "A policeman came back and knelt down on the driveway. He tried to pry my fingers from the gun. And he started crying and said, 'I'm gonna break your fingers. I can't get them loose.' But I couldn't let go of the handle. My knuckles were swollen up, I was holding it so tight. The grip I had on that gun was what kept my attacker from getting it from me. Even as big a man as he was, he couldn't take it away."

After the gun was finally extracted, an officer persuaded Foust to move to an ambulance waiting up the street.

She noticed that everybody who looked at her winced. Under their breaths, she heard them cursing her attacker. Later, at the hospital, she managed to find a mirror. It was only then that she understood their reactions.

The canine units finally arrived.

Police moved in behind the dogs. Inside they found knocked over tables, broken chairs, and shattered dishes on the floor. The bloody walls and floors attested to the desperate struggle that had taken place in the dining room and master bedroom.

As paramedics tended her wounds, Foust heard the dispatcher's terse messages crackling over the radio. Much of the conversation was in code, so she didn't understand what was being said.

It seemed that every police officer not directly involved in the search of the house dropped by to try to cheer her up. They stood around the back of the ambulance asking the paramedics if she was going to make it.

"The ambulance people were talking about whether or not my attacker was dead. One said, 'We'll know in a minute.' And then over the radio there came a call for a 'Code-6 Ambulance.' Outside, the place erupted with cheers. They told me that 'Code 6' meant they were picking up a body."

The first officers to enter the house found the invader stretched out in the doorway between the master bedroom and the dining room. He still wore a stocking mask and his makeshift gloves. Paramedics examined him and found four bullet wounds. The medical examiner later concluded that the first shot had entered his mouth; the second shot had hit him in the heart; the third shot was to the abdomen; and the fourth bullet hit him in the groin.

Before Sammie Foust was transported to the hospital, police officers and paramedics dropped by to thank her for killing such a vicious predator.

"Why would you thank me for that?" she asked.

A patrolman's comment seemed to speak for them all. "If he

attacked my wife or my daughter, they'd be dead. There's no way they could have survived such an attack."

Foust still recalls being wheeled into the emergency room at Cape Coral Hospital. "It was close to Mother's Day, and all I could think about was that I had killed some mother's son. Because as bad as your children might be, you still love them."

A medical team examined Foust and explained the physical damage that she had incurred. Her attacker had knocked out four of her teeth, which she'd swallowed. The bones in her gums were crushed, and her left cheekbone was fractured. An eyeball was hanging out of its socket. Her nose was broken, and her larynx fractured. The good news was that the cuts made by the knife were superficial.

Foust was rushed to a nearby eye clinic. Her eye was surgically reattached and permanent damage was minimal.

Later, Foust met Cape Coral Police Department Victim's Advocate, Pat Lucas. Foust has nothing but praise for Lucas and the Cape Coral Police Department.

● ● ●

The attack on Sammie Foust had lasted for nearly an hour. Her assailant was identified as James Wayne Horne.

With nearly thirty arrests, he had been through the Florida state prison system three times. Only a few weeks before, Horne had been released after serving slightly more than one year of a ten-year sentence for aggravated assault. He'd beaten a police officer while being arrested for a crime identical to the one he committed against Foust.

Horne had recently moved to Cape Coral, continuing a drug habit he'd developed years earlier. An autopsy report stated that he had crack cocaine in his system when he broke into Foust's home.

Investigators concluded that Horne had met someone whom Foust had once assisted. Although no one was ever charged, they believed this person had told Horne that Foust was a divorcée who lived alone. Police speculated that the crack addict had decided to break into her house, force her to give him any money she had, then murder her and steal anything else he thought he could sell.

• • •

"Fear," Sammie Foust said, "is something you dread, like when you're trying to cross a street and see a truck roaring at you. Horror is what just happened. Like after the truck hits you. Horror is what I felt when that man was beating on me."

Foust went through a year of counseling, but she now has exhausted the funds she was using to pay for a psychiatrist. She still has unresolved emotional issues to deal with and sits alone in her home dreading to hear the doorbell ring.

Medical bills from the physical injuries suffered in the attack have left her financially strapped. She has not been able to have her gums and teeth properly repaired and can only eat soft food.

Insensitive people have also added to her withdrawal from society. One home repairman brought his son with him to do a job. "Look at the woman who shot that man in the balls," he told his son. Foust immediately asked them to leave.

She struggles to make sense of the unprovoked, vicious attack.

"The Fort Myers newspaper put out an article on gun control," she said recently. "The headlines of one column said, 'Woman owes her life to gun.' I say that headline should be, 'Woman owes her life to God, and her conviction that she had the right to fight for her life.'

"I owe my life to the strength God gave me, and one thing He gave me was the good fortune to have a gun. Still, I haven't figured out why God kept me alive. I don't ask why this happened. What I do ask is why God kept me alive."

She concluded the interview by saying, "If there's one reason God kept me alive, it may be to tell others to find the strength within themselves to fight. To say, *My life is worth fighting for.*"

A final irony is that although Foust regretted killing "some mother's son," no one showed up to claim his body.

James Wayne Horne was buried at county expense.

5

Orlando: Magic Kingdom or the New Dodge City?

"An Orange County robbery suspect Tuesday became the ninth gunman in 18 months to die at the hands of an intended victim. . . ."
—Orlando Sentinel, January 31, 1996

The sign bolted to the window of the Fort Pitt Grocery & Coin Laundry should have been enough to cause the masked man to rethink his plan. It read: WARNING. ROBBERY STAKEOUT AREA. VIOLATORS WILL BE DISARMED BY FORCE.

At 7:50 P.M., January 29, 1996, darkness had long since fallen. Frances Postlethwait stood behind the counter at the cash register, "counting the numbers and getting ready to close," as she later remarked. She was looking forward to getting home to her husband and son.

A second clerk, Darlene Smith, stood a few feet away, matching stock on hand with invoice records.

In an office behind the counter, Sam Turrisi sat at his desk completing the day's paperwork. His parents had built a small, one-room grocery store back in 1923. Old photographs show a sandy trail running alongside a solitary frame structure. Orlando, Florida, had grown mightily since then.

Over the years, the city had closed in on the little store. Numerous additions had been made to keep up with the times, including the Laundromat on the side. And a new living area with office space had been built in the back.

Sam Turrisi joined the army just weeks after America entered World War II. Some eight months later, he found himself serving as a crew member in the old Army Air Corps—flying supplies in to Merrill's marauders.

The Burma campaign was unsurpassed in viciousness and hardship. It had begun with Japanese victories and Allied humiliation and retreat, compounded by widespread Japanese torture and murder of prisoners, soldier and civilian alike. But the Allies regrouped under hard men like Lt. Colonel Frank Merrill and British Brigadier "Mad" Mike Calvert.

Those soldiers began to take back Burma inch-by-inch, man-to-man, in some of the fiercest hand-to-hand fighting the world has ever seen.

Turrisi's duties were to help resupply the troops and fly out the wounded. During the summer of 1944, the weary pilots and crews were averaging an incredible three hundred hours a month in the air, making runs in the worst weather imaginable. But they never failed to respond.

After the war, Turrisi reenlisted in the army, serving a total of eight years. Later, he transferred to the newly formed United States Air Force, where he added fifteen more.

During this tenure, he often represented the air force in shooting competitions throughout the world. The medals that hang on his wall attest to his marksmanship.

Turrisi retired from active duty twenty-three years after going off to war. He returned to Orlando and took over the operation of the family-owned business.

On that night of January 29, 1996, he was adding up ledger columns on his calculator. The door to the grocery store opened, triggering a high-pitched squeal from an alarm in his office.

Out on the floor, Postlethwait looked up and the color drained from her face.

A man rushed toward the counter.

He was dressed in black, with a baseball cap sagging low on his forehead. Oversize aviator sunglasses glinted in the lights. A camouflage bandanna covered the lower part of his face.

But what alarmed Postlethwait most was the silver gun he held in his hand.

"Get on the floor!"

Postlethwait sank to her knees directly beneath the cash register.

"Gimme your money!" the robber shouted. He threw a plastic bag over the counter. As it fluttered to the floor, Postlethwait grabbed it.

She saw the man bend over the barrier and felt the steel barrel as he pressed the gun against her temple.

Reflexively, she screamed.

"Shut up!" the gunman commanded.

From off to her left, her coworker Darlene Smith yelled, "Give him the money, Frances."

"Make it quick!" the robber demanded.

The gunman was barrel-chested and breathing heavily.

With her right hand, Postlethwait reached above the counter to open the register. Unable to see the keys, she blindly punched at them with her fingers. Immediately she knew she'd hit the wrong digits.

Now the register was jammed.

"Gimme your money or you're dead!" The robber spoke rapidly, with a resounding harshness that added urgency to his threats.

"*Give* him the money, Frances."

The robber punched at Postlethwait's face with the gun. His shouts were getting louder. Postlethwait was in a life-or-death predicament. If she stood up to try to reprogram the register, he might shoot her. But if she continued to cower beneath the counter, she would never be able to open it.

From his office, Turrisi heard screaming. Although it was totally out of character for both women, he thought they might be arguing.

Whatever was going on, he intended to set things straight.

Turrisi wheeled his executive chair to the door, looked through, and was about to instruct the employees to calm down when he spotted the robber.

The man was leaning over the counter holding a gun in Postlethwait's face, demanding that she fill the bag with large bills. The clerk knelt beneath the register, trying to open it with one hand, while she begged the gunman not to shoot her.

The robber's focus was one-dimensional. He did not see Turrisi.

The grocer became a stalker now, like the marksman he'd been during the war. He quietly rolled his chair back out of sight. Rising

Above: *Sam Turrisi holding "Old Slabsides," the .45 he used to defend himself and his employees during an armed robbery at his grocery store on January 29, 1996.* Below: *Frances Postlethwait, a clerk at the Fort Pitt Grocery & Coin Laundry.*

on steady legs, he moved to the closet. On the top shelf lay a .45 caliber semiautomatic pistol, Model 1911. He'd bought it in 1953 and had used it for target practice behind his store until the city grew too close for him to safely shoot there.

Approved by the Secretary of War in 1911 as America's official armed services sidearm, "Old Slabsides," as the .45 was affectionately called by the troops, was retired from duty in 1985. Today it is still the most respected and copied handgun design in the world.

Now, as he'd been taught in the military, Turrisi kept five rounds in the magazine, none in the barrel. That way, some shooters maintain, an automatic has less chance of jamming. Turrisi picked up the pistol, chambered a shell, and stepped quietly toward the robbery in progress. His intention was to protect his clerks and himself; then, if possible, to apprehend the gunman.

Postlethwait still had not been able to open the cash drawer.

Things were going from bad to worse.

"Give him the money, Frances," Smith pleaded. "He's gonna kill us."

"Please don't shoot," Postlethwait begged. "I'm trying to give you the money." She couldn't think of anything else to say.

The robber's hand was steady as he placed the barrel of the gun on the top of her head.

He said, very quietly this time, "This is it, lady. Put the cash in the bag or you're dead!"

Postlethwait knew then that she was about to die. She began screaming, trying to pull away from the gun.

Before stepping into the line of fire, Turrisi unlatched the safety on his .45.

The grocer moved into the open. He aimed at the robber's heart and yelled, "Drop your gun."

The action seemed to slow down, like a video played in slow motion. Postlethwait's screams provided an eerie soundtrack for what was about to come.

"Drop your gun!" Turrisi repeated.

The robber looked up, uncertain, then swung his weapon toward Turrisi.

The sharpshooter had done this so many times that his response was almost routine.

Boom!

The .45 jerked back, its recoil snapping his hand into the air.

The robber stood as if frozen in space. Then he staggered backward. He tried to raise his gun as Turrisi held his firearm in place, ready to fire again. Then the gunman collapsed to the floor.

Frances Postlethwait and Darlene Smith crawled frantically away. Once inside Turrisi's office, keeping her head beneath the counter, Smith grabbed the telephone.

"There's been a shooting at the Fort Pitt Grocery Store. Please get someone here." Her voice was calm, but a thousand yellow jackets were swarming through her body.

Turrisi moved around the counter. The robber was on his belly, pulling himself to the door.

Turrisi noticed he'd dropped his weapon. It lay on the floor near the counter.

"If you've got another gun on you, I'm gonna shoot you again," Turrisi told the robber.

"No, man. Please!" The downed man flinched, then resumed dragging himself toward the door.

Suddenly, a movement behind the bread counter drew Turrisi's attention. Did the robber have an accomplice? he wondered.

"Come on out, or I'll shoot you, too!" Turrisi said.

A tremulous voice stammered, "I'm just a customer!"

A man stepped from behind the counter holding a loaf of bread and a carton of milk. He'd been shopping when the holdup began and thought it best to remain concealed.

His face paled when he saw the .45 aimed at his face.

"Don't shoot, man," he repeated. "I'm just a customer."

"Then get the hell out of here!" Turrisi growled.

The customer rushed out with his groceries, stumbling over the wounded holdup man who was still struggling to reach the exit.

Far away, Turrisi heard the welcome sound of sirens.

"Every cop in Orlando was here five seconds after we called," Turrisi said later.

Until they determined that he'd shot an armed robber, detectives from the Orange County Sheriff's Department treated Turrisi as a suspect.

"But I done it by the book," he said, "and there's nothing they could charge me with."

Indeed, Orange County Sheriff's Commander Steve Jones later stated, "We don't anticipate any charges. Mr. Turrisi did what he had to do. They were in fear for their lives."

● ● ●

Gilbert Ayala died three hours after being shot by Sam Turrisi. The former marksman had put a .45 slug just below the heart.

For weeks, Turrisi was treated like a hero. Citizens stopped by his store just to buy something from the man who fought back. One supporter came from clear across town to hand him a one-dollar bill.

"What's that for?" Turrisi asked.

"I want to be a part of this," the man told him. "The dollar bill is to pay for the bullet you used to shoot that son of a bitch."

When Francis Postlethwait went to a supermarket to cash her check, the cashier noted that it was from the Fort Pitt Grocery & Coin Laundry.

"Don't even show me any ID," he said. "If it bounces, I'll cover it."

The customer who was in the store selecting groceries at the time of the robbery returned the next day and insisted on paying for the items he'd fled with.

An investigation revealed that Ayala had held up two convenience stores earlier in the week.

In a recent interview, Sam Turrisi gave his opinion of the crime problem.

"They're not hard enough on these criminals. When you take guns away, you're taking them away from the good citizens. [Criminals] don't buy guns, they steal them. So you're just disarming the good people. I heard through the grapevine later on that Ayala had stolen the pistol he used to try to rob me.

"I don't have any regrets. I'd do it again tomorrow."

• • •

Lillie Mae Ponder, 74, and her wheelchair-bound husband, Paul, lived on Lenox Boulevard near the Ivey Lane public housing project. The neighborhood has the highest rate of criminal activity in Orlando.

On December 6, 1994, Ponder returned home from church to find her residence had been burglarized. Paul Ponder reported that he had heard noises coming from an adjacent room, but was unable to investigate because of his feeble condition. Lillie Mae told responding officers that two vacuum cleaners, a portable radio, and a set of hair clippers were missing. There was no sign of forced entry. Officers advised the Ponders to keep their doors locked.

Just a few hours later, at 1:15 A.M., Lillie Mae was awakened by noises in the back of the house. She and her husband slept in separate bedrooms, and his screams told her he was being attacked. She pulled a .38 Special from a cardboard box where she kept it hidden. Then she proceeded to check out the disturbance.

In the bedroom, an intruder was pointing a spray can at her husband. Paul was thrashing on the bed as he tried to keep his face covered by his hands. The assailant was methodically spraying Paul's exposed facial areas with Mace.

Lillie Mae smelled the chemical first, then felt her eyes start to burn.

That was when the intruder turned to her.

Blasting her full in the face, he laughed as she shrieked.

With her eyes on fire, and the chemicals choking her, Ponder pointed the gun toward the sound of the laughter.

She fired three times. The small room rang with the gunshots. At first, Lillie Mae was afraid she'd hit Paul. But then she heard the intruder fall and ran from the room to dial 911.

Upon arrival, police found the burglar dead in Paul's bedroom. He had been hit in the head and died instantly. Investigators found he'd broken into the house through a locked window near the back entrance.

An investigating officer said, "She shot at him two or three times, and this was after she'd been maced. So it was kind of a lucky shot."

The shooting was ruled justifiable homicide.

• • •

At 11:41 P.M., February 5, 1995, Raymond Scott had just gone to bed. His 20-year-old son and teenage daughter played video games in the living room, while Scott's girlfriend, Yvette Sharpe, was in the kitchen.

The family lived in the Park Central Apartments on Texas Avenue in Orlando. They had spent most of that day, a Sunday, lounging around the pool. Monday morning the adults had to go back to work.

Just minutes before, a stranger had knocked on the door. When Sharpe answered, the woman asked if "Donna" lived there. Sharpe told her no, and the woman praised Sharpe's pretty jewelry. It seemed a strange response, and Sharpe was still puzzled by the incident.

Suddenly, she heard a crash.

As she turned, she saw the door disintegrate in a cloud of smoke. Two men wearing black ski masks and waving guns jumped in out of the haze.

"Get down on the floor!" they screamed in unison.

Sharpe saw one of the invaders run to Scott's children. He covered them with his gun.

"Lay down!" he screamed.

They did as they were told. The gunman began to fumble with a roll of black electrical tape. He's going to tie their hands, Sharpe thought. What's going to happen next?

Before she could respond, the second invader rushed at her. Pushing her to the floor, he yelled, "Stay down." He pointed a gun at her face. Sharpe begged him not to hurt anyone.

Scott had been dozing when he heard the door burst open.

He reached for the 9 mm automatic that he kept beside the bed. Then he crept to the door and peered out. In the living room, a masked man was attempting to bind his son's hands.

Scott pushed the door open and came out firing. His first bullet drove the masked intruder away from his children. But after backing off a step, the gunman took time to return fire. Scott charged into the room, firing a volley that sent the invader fleeing out the door.

Suddenly Scott was attacked by the second gunman.

After a shot whizzed by his face, the home owner turned to the accomplice and fired. Scott and his assailant exchanged gunfire before the gunman ran out the door. As he hit the doorway, Scott noticed the gunman stumble.

Scott raced after him, continuing to fire until his gun was empty.

He returned to find his apartment reeking of burnt gunpowder.

He could barely see through the gunsmoke. His son, daughter, and girlfriend were all hysterical, trembling as they tried to hug him.

"Call 911," he said, and his daughter ran to the telephone.

Responding officers arrested a wounded suspect, Stephen LeRoy Jones, when he called them from Orlando Regional Medical Center and claimed to have been involved in a robbery at a local Winn-Dixie. Detectives found that his story didn't match, and under interrogation he quickly confessed to being involved in the home invasion. At the hospital he was treated for a bullet wound to the elbow. There he was arrested for armed burglary.

After identifying the second gunman, police began a canvas of the neighborhood for Shonrell J. Harper. At 7:30 A.M. the following morning, his body was discovered under a stairway at the apartment complex. Beneath his body lay a bloody ski mask, and his outstretched hands held a roll of electrical tape.

"This was a pure and simple home invasion," said a spokesperson for the Orange County Sheriff's Department.

Investigators uncovered a bizarre plot to rob Sharpe of her jewelry. Jones, Harper, and an accomplice, Autumn Jackson, had spent the day at the apartment swimming pool looking for someone to rob. Yvette Sharpe was chosen because of the flashy gold necklaces and rings she wore.

Jackson was dispatched to make sure the intended victims were asleep. She knocked on the door and was surprised when Sharpe answered. After reporting this to Jones and Harper, they decided that she was the only party awake in the house. So they kicked the door down. The idea was to burst in and neutralize the male occupants before they could get out of their beds.

Both Jackson and Jones were later charged with additional crimes, including armed burglary, armed robbery, and second degree murder. (In Florida, a participant can be charged with murder if an accomplice dies during the commission of a felony.)

Raymond Scott was not charged.

•••

When Gilbert Ayala decided to rob Sam Turrisi's Fort Pitt Grocery, he paid with his life for violating a principle long passed around in prisons throughout the United States: leave "mom-and-pop" grocery stores alone!

In a 1996 study conducted by the Athena Research Institute in Seattle, Washington, 310 armed robbers were interviewed about their tactics when committing their crimes. The consensus among those convicts was to rob chain stores exclusively, because franchise policies almost universally prohibit firearms on the premises. A sole proprietor, however, has no board of directors; after all, it's often his only source of income. Many times he or she will protect it to the last cartridge.

Sam Turrisi is an example of such an owner. He grew up in Orlando in the 1920s and 1930s. He feels that crime is out of control, and that citizens must protect themselves. Interviews with local citizens support that view.

Orlando, Florida, is a microcosm of America. True, there are the well-known Disney theme parks, and other attractions, including the Orlando Magic professional basketball team. The Houston Astros spring training camp is in nearby Kissimmee, and there are thousands of hotels and restaurants that cater to the tourists.

But beneath the glitter are the working men and women who hold the place together. Some are native Floridians, some transplants from other parts of the country, and a high percentage are foreigners looking to achieve the American dream. Cubans, Indians, and Asians are frequently found working in restaurants, clothing stores, and tourist attractions in the area.

These are the people that crime happens to, and the people who are most likely to fight back when attacked. They understand that the police will not be there when they are assaulted, robbed, or threatened. To survive, they must protect themselves. It is these people, more than any other group, who are armed.

Many are quick to say that politicians are a gutless breed who have allowed criminals to go unpunished. When convicted of vicious crimes, the punishment these offenders receive is outrageously lenient. Had the political system worked as it should, they say, there would be no parole, no early release, no halfway houses. Criminals would be tried, convicted, and sent away to prison to serve out their full terms. Many refer to Florida's correctional system as "turnstile justice."

Because of these sentiments, Florida voters recently approved the ballot initiative, in which citizens can place constitutional amendments on the ballot in statewide elections. Thus, citizens can override the apathetic politicians and make their own laws. Predictably, longer sentences and fewer appeals have been a priority.

6

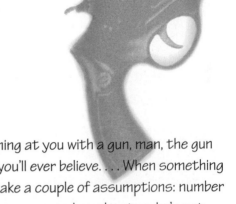

Crack Shot

"When you see a guy coming at you with a gun, man, the gun stands out like nothing you'll ever believe.... When something like that happens, you make a couple of assumptions: number one, he's not selling newspapers, and number two, he's not trying to ask for a ride across town."
—*Jim Eichelberg*

At a little past 5:00 A.M., February 19, 1997, Jimmy Barber pulled his pickup truck into the Chevron gas station at the intersection of Milwee Street and Highway 290. Most of Houston, Texas, was still asleep as Barber walked around the back of his truck to the pump.

As he stuck the nozzle in the gas tank, he felt the barrel of a gun press against his temple.

Turning toward his assailant, Barber saw a man with a dark jacket holding a .357 Magnum. He wondered how he'd missed seeing the man. By then it was too late.

"Hand me your wallet!" the man said. Barber complied.

"Now your keys!"

Barber reached into his pocket. Several dozen keys jingled on the ring as he handed them over. Barber's assailant walked around the pickup and opened the front door.

Jimmy Barber needed no further invitation. He took to his heels and fled into the darkness. The gunman ignored the fleeing victim. He climbed into the truck and stuck a key in the ignition.

It was the wrong one.

He tried another. And another. The gunman couldn't find the right key.

He cursed and stepped out of the truck.

He still needed a ride.

● ● ●

Jim Eichelberg had begun work at four o'clock that morning. Each day he got up before daylight to replenish the machines of his vending business.

During a recent interview, Eichelberg stated, "It's a nice time to work." He beat the morning rush-hour traffic, and he was able to buy his vending products, which were then placed in the machines.

The businesses liked the arrangement as well. "It's like having a phantom service person come in and fill the machines," he said. "I take care of them, fix them, maintain them. I have everything done before anybody shows up."

At approximately 5:45 that February morning, Eichelberg was traveling east on Milwee Street. He'd driven to Vend-O-Matic, bought bakery goods, and was heading toward Highway 290.

Jim Eichelberg with his 1985 Ford Custom van that he uses to transport goods for his vending machine business.

The intersection of Milwee Street and Highway 290 near the site of the attempted car-jacking. The Chevron gas station can be seen beyond the stop sign.

He drove a 1985 Ford Custom van. Eichelberg had pulled out all unnecessary accessories in order to outfit it for his business. That morning he was hauling several machines that he hoped to install at local businesses. He was also carrying about two thousand dollars in cash.

The speed limit on Milwee was twenty miles per hour. It was a rough, poorly paved road with one faint streetlight stuck square in the middle of the block.

Eichelberg drove past the back exit of the Chevron gas station and noticed a pedestrian heading east on the north side of the road. The man was on the driver's side of Eichelberg's van. The distributor had never seen anyone there at that time of the morning, so he took special notice of this man.

When he reached Highway 290, the light was red. He pulled to a stop, then looked in his side mirror again. This time he didn't see anybody.

Thinking back on the incident, Eichelberg said, "I looked out my right mirror and saw this guy running behind my truck. He'd run across the street behind the van and was coming up on the right side. Because that streetlight was halfway down the block, it just so happened that I saw a flash off the gun."

A year earlier, Eichelberg had applied for a permit to carry a concealed weapon, or what Texans call a "carry permit." He'd undergone an extensive background investigation as well as many hours of classroom and field training, and had paid nearly two hundred and fifty dollars for a license. The training he'd received on the pistol range was about to save his life.

Eichelberg's handgun lay on the floor, wedged somewhere

between the driver's seat and the passenger side. It was a Smith & Wesson five-shot .38 revolver—a small, light weapon that was easily concealed.

It took a couple of seconds for him to fully realize that the man was running after his van. This was the sort of thing that happens on television, or to someone else. Eichelberg took precious seconds to fumble through the clutter between the seats. He dislodged some old files and a jacket before his fingers felt the grip of the handgun.

It was almost too late.

"It took three seconds for me to dig the gun out, and three seconds for this guy to get to the door." The aggressor was staring at him through the window, not more than a foot away. Suddenly, he pointed the gun at Eichelberg's face and began screaming at him. Because the window was rolled up, Eichelberg couldn't understand what the gunman was saying.

His first instinct was to gun the accelerator and speed away, but even at 5:45 in the morning, all the lanes of Highway 290 were jammed with traffic. He couldn't pull out. He didn't think to back up.

Eichelberg picked up his pistol and pointed it at the window. "I figured he was there for no good," Eichelberg said. "So I shot through the closed window. I got a real good look at him because there was enough light coming from traffic to light up his face and the gun."

When Eichelberg fired, the glass shattered.

His assailant disappeared. Eichelberg was afraid he'd missed, and that the man was going to start shooting into the van.

Eichelberg shut off the engine, stepped out, and started to run west on Milwee.

Though badly shaken, he still had the presence of mind to take his pistol with him.

He intended to run to the Chevron gas station half a block away and find a pay phone.

As he ran past the back of his van, Eichelberg came face to face with the gunman. They stopped and stared at each other, only six feet apart.

Before he could duck, the attacker aimed his gun at Eichelberg's head and pulled the trigger. The shot missed, but the sound jarred Eichelberg's eardrums. The assailant's weapon was also a .357 Magnum. To Eichelberg, it sounded like a sonic boom when it went off.

Eichelberg raised his pistol and fired. The gunman twisted away from the shot and jumped across a ditch.

Now Eichelberg was exposed beneath the streetlight, while his assailant had apparently decided to flee into the darkness. Eichelberg briefly considered chasing the gunman but decided instead to stand his ground where he could see. Let the police department track the madman down.

As the gunman ran deeper into the woods, he abruptly stopped. About twenty feet away, he whipped around toward Eichelberg and fired again.

Eichelberg saw the muzzle flash from his gun. As he stated, "It's straight out of the class you take when you get your carry permit. You shoot at silhouettes. When he fired there was a perfect silhouette lighted up from the muzzle flash and side flash from his revolver. I pointed my gun in the direction that the fire flash had come from, and I pulled the trigger."

Pressing his luck, Eichelberg continued to stand his ground beneath the streetlight. He saw another muzzle flash from his assailant's gun and fired again. He wasn't looking down the sights on the barrel of the gun, because he couldn't see them.

"He shot five times and I shot five times," Eichelberg remembered. He'd traded the gunman bullet for bullet and was surprised to find himself untouched.

But now he had an empty gun and was standing under the light where the assailant could see him.

The next few moments were uncertain ones for Eichelberg as he tried to decide on a course of action. The gas station behind him would be a perfect place for an ambush. His attacker might have circled back and could be waiting there. Or he might still be out in the darkness reloading his weapon. So Eichelberg chose to make for his van. It was the safest haven he could think of just then.

He darted across the road, jumped in, and drove through the red light. From the lights of oncoming cars, he saw bits of shattered glass lying on the seat. The slivers sparkled like small diamonds, and, on a larger shard, Eichelberg discerned a reddish tint.

He surmised that he'd hit the suspect with at least one shot.

Eichelberg managed to squeeze into the flow of traffic and drive to the next exit, where he saw the lights of a Shell gas station. He pulled up to the window but found no one inside. The station wasn't open yet.

In the rear was a pay telephone. Eichelberg hesitated. He desperately needed to call the police, but his attacker seemed to be everywhere. Bullets had failed to stop him, and the man's game plan was beyond Eichelberg's comprehension.

After considering his options, Eichelberg reluctantly got out and called 911, reporting the facts to the dispatcher as well as he could recall. Then he prepared himself for when the police would arrive.

As instructed in the concealed permit carry classes, Eichelberg found a spot beneath a street lamp. There he clasped his hands on his head, holding both his permit-to-carry license and driver's license. The reason for doing this, according to his firearms instructors, was to appear to responding officers as nonthreatening as possible. Police sometimes mistake victims for criminals.

The first officer to arrive ignored Eichelberg's nonthreatening posture. He brusquely asked where the assailant had been last sighted, then sped away. A second officer also drove up and asked where the assailant had last been seen. He, too, sped off. By then, Eichelberg was beginning to feel a little foolish standing beneath the floodlight with his hands on his head.

A third police officer drove up and threw the door open.

"Get in," he shouted. "You got him." Before complying, Eichelberg said, "I've got money and product in my truck. It's sitting here in front of a gas station with the window blown out, and there's a gun on the seat."

The officer responded, "I'll take the gun and get someone to stand guard over the truck."

Another officer arrived in less than five minutes, and Eichelberg's van was wrapped in crime-scene tape. "That officer literally sat there in front of it the rest of the night and into the next day, guarding it," Eichelberg recounted.

Eichelberg was driven to a Stop 'n' Go convenience store on the corner of Antoine and 34th Street. A bloody trail slithered down the sidewalk to the front door.

The gunman was lying a foot from the entrance. He was identified as James Turner.

An officer asked if the downed man was his attacker. Eichelberg had no trouble identifying him, but something seemed different. His jacket and black cap were missing.

"Help me," the attacker moaned. "Somebody shot me." His speech was fast, slurred and shrill, like somebody gargling a mouthful of crickets.

"Somebody shot me," Turner repeated.

The officer chuckled and said, "We know, we've got the guy who shot you right here." The officer added, "Oh, by the way, I arrested you two years ago for possession of crack. Didn't I tell you to stay off that stuff?"

Turner could bleed no more. He'd lost so much that there was little blood left in his body. His vital signs were negligible, and his eyes rolled randomly around in their sockets.

Waiting for an ambulance, officers counted six gunshot wounds.

The first shot, the one through the window, had hit Turner two inches above the heart—embedded in the wound were slivers of broken glass. Bullets had also passed through both thighs, his groin, and his right hand. And a bullet was lodged in the right cheek of his buttocks. Doctors later determined that one of the rounds had gone into his hand, exited, and then pierced his groin. "That's how you get six shots out of a five-shot revolver," one of the arresting officers explained.

When the ambulance arrived, paramedics flipped Turner onto his stomach. A crack pipe tumbled out of his pocket, along with several rocks of cocaine.

As a final indignity, arresting officers handcuffed the almost lifeless assailant before the ambulance took him to Ben Taub Hospital.

By now, detectives had arrived.

The lead investigator asked Eichelberg, "Where's his gun?"

"I don't know," Eichelberg said. "But I'm telling you he shot at me five times."

The cop was becoming suspicious.

"Hey, what's the deal here?" he asked. "You described him as wearing a dark jacket and cap."

Eichelberg reiterated that the description he'd called in was what he'd seen.

A few minutes later, a deputy walked up holding a dark jacket. "I found this back behind the convenience store," he said. Winking at Eichelberg, he said to the detective, "Check out what's in it."

The investigator used rubber gloves to open the jacket. Inside was a .357 Magnum. Fingerprints in blood were stained all over the handle.

"Is this the gun he used?"

Eichelberg nodded. "Looks like it."

Another officer walked up. He held a black cap that he'd found in the driveway of the Stop 'n' Go.

An officer introduced Eichelberg to a shaken and disheveled Jimmy Barber. "He was hiding in the ditch during the entire gunfight," the officer said. "He confirmed everything you told us."

The vending machine business owner maintains that in his dealings with the police department, he was shown every courtesy. He said, "Since I had a carry permit, the police treated me like royalty. They treated me as nice as anybody could: Do you want something to drink? they asked. Do you need to call someone and tell them you're not coming in to work?

"They gave us both [Eichelberg and Jimmy Barber] a ride to the Homicide Division, which is on the south side of town. There they took statements from both of us. They kept us until about noon, then took us back to the scene. By this time, my wife had called a wrecker and had them bring the van home, and she made arrangements to get the window fixed."

Eichelberg stated, "Jimmy Barber's keys were in Turner's pocket, and they were returned to him by police. When I saw them, I laughed out loud. Barber has one of these three-inch-diameter key rings with a hundred keys on it. Turner was so high on crack he couldn't find the key to fit the ignition. That's why he chose me, I suppose. He was looking for a ride."

• • •

Further investigation led police to present the following scenario of the events of that morning.

James Turner had been smoking crack with acquaintances most of the night. He'd stolen the .357 Magnum from one of his street friends and was taking it to his girlfriend's house to conceal it there. At some point during his journey, he realized that her house was several miles away. He decided to commandeer a vehicle.

When he saw Barber fueling his vehicle, he decided to take it.

After stealing the keys to Barber's truck, Turner never found the ignition key among the scores on the giant ring. He finally succumbed to frustration, jumped out of the truck, and tried to find Barber. He planned to force the victim to come back and start the truck for him. But Barber had vanished in the darkness.

Turner was now fixated on finding a vehicle to drive to his girl-friend's house. So when he saw Jim Eichelberg sitting at the stop-light, waiting to cross Highway 290, Turner thought he'd found his ride. All he had to do was sneak up on the motorist, wave his Magnum, and trade places with the driver. And, for good measure, the keys were already in the ignition.

But Eichelberg had seen him, and before he could car-jack the van, the motorist shot him.

Across the street, Barber watched in the darkness. He rolled into a ditch at the first shot and hid there as the scene unfolded.

Turner, in his drugged haze, didn't realize he'd been shot in the chest.

When Eichelberg leaped from the van in an attempt to flee, Turner followed him. His new plan was to run Eichelberg down, kill him, and take his keys.

But cocaine rendered him a remarkably poor shot. Even though he took careful aim with each shot, Turner never came close.

Eichelberg, on the other hand, had received hours of training, and knew what to do in case he was attacked.

He made quick work of Turner.

• • •

James Turner fully recovered from his wounds, and a trial date was set for November 1997. Charged with the aggravated assault of Eichelberg, Turner had previously pleaded guilty to the armed robbery of Jimmy Barber.

More was at stake, though, than the charge of aggravated assault on Jim Eichelberg. Because Turner was a convicted felon with multiple convictions—and free on parole when he attempted the car-jackings—he faced the consequences of a recent revision to the Texas criminal code: if convicted, he would have to serve at least half of any sentence the court might impose. And the district attorney's office was seeking a very stiff sentence.

Not surprisingly, James Turner pleaded innocent.

His first hurdle in surmounting the charge was to devise a plausible defense. Turner's version of the events of that night was noteworthy for its creativity, if not for its credibility.

"That guy over there, Jimmy Barber, tried to rob me when I walked by the gas pump," Turner explained to the court. "I fired all my bullets up in the air just to scare him away, right there by the gas pumps."

The prosecution called a police officer to rebut Turner's testimony. The officer stated that a huge monolithic canopy overhung all of the gas pumps, and no bullet holes were present. He submitted photographs to back up his testimony, and these were placed into evidence.

Jimmy Barber also testified. He swore under oath that he had never tried to rob the defendant. Furthermore, he'd witnessed the entire incident involving Eichelberg and Turner, and stated that Turner had been the unprovoked aggressor from beginning to end.

But there was more to come from Turner.

Eichelberg, according to the defense, was actually a freelance vigilante who roamed the streets of Harris County seeking unfortunate victims to execute. Eichelberg had seen Turner fire his gun into the air, so he knew the defendant was carrying an empty firearm. Consequently, the vigilante shot Turner six times as he tried to escape.

The prosecuting attorney destroyed, point by point, Turner's testimony. For example, the defendant suffered five frontal gunshot wounds but only one to the back area of his body.

When the jury retired to consider the charges, Turner appeared to be upbeat about his chances for acquittal.

The jury teased him. They stayed out all day. Defendants know that the longer a jury is out, the better chance there is for acquittal—or a hung jury. However, this was not to be for James Turner.

When the jurors finally returned to the courtroom, they brought with them a verdict of guilty. If Turner's spirits weren't dashed by then, the trial judge sentenced him to consecutive twenty-five-year sentences for the aggravated robbery of Barber and the aggravated assault of Eichelberg. Additionally, Turner was found to be a career criminal. He will have to serve at least twenty-five years before he is eligible for parole.

• • •

Right-to-carry laws differ in each state.

Texas has one of the most stringent laws in the country. The state fee alone is $140. Classroom tuition costs another $100.

Range time is required, in which the applicant can score up to 250 points. A written test and an FBI background check complete the process.

"It takes a while, it's expensive, and it's worth it," Eichelberg said. "When you have a carry permit, you have all the authority of a peace officer. In Texas, you can actually detain someone. You can stop a third party from attacking a second party without their permission. You can get involved in a theft of your neighbor's property, anything that a peace officer can do. Also, the study of Texas law that goes along with getting a permit is worth gold. And you have to learn it, or you don't pass."

In Texas, a concealed weapon means just that. If the profile of a gun is showing in your pocket, you can lose your license.

The history of modern right-to-carry laws dates back to 1987. Before that time, citizens who wanted to obtain a license to carry a firearm were required to apply to the local police chief or county sheriff. Unfortunately, most police officials were hostile to the law. For instance, in Los Angeles, from 1984 to 1992, the city refused to issue a single permit.

In Denver, the police chief issued only forty-five permits during the entire decade of the 1980s. When talk show host Alan Berg applied for a permit because of numerous death threats, he was denied. An official stated, "Fearing for your life is not a compelling reason to have a permit." A few months later, Berg was gunned down at his home.

In 1987, in response to a series of brutal murders, Florida passed the first right-to-carry law in the nation. The key feature was that the state *must* grant the permit as soon as any citizen satisfied objective licensing criteria. In Florida, there would be no police officials making subjective decisions on who got a permit.

Opponents predicted a bloodbath on the streets, and the law was closely monitored. Between October 1987, and April 1992, 221,443 permits were issued. During that time, only eighteen gun crimes were committed by licensed carriers. And the homicide rate in that state plummeted 21 percent.

Florida's law has become a model for other states.

In the Sunshine state, the cost to apply is $85, plus small miscellaneous charges. Fingerprints are required, as well as a background check. The law states that a license is to be issued if: (1) the applicant is at least 21 and a resident of the both the U.S. and the state of Florida; (2) does not suffer physical infirmity that prevents safe handling of a firearm; (3) is not a convicted felon; (4) has not been convicted of a crime of violence or drug offense within the last three years; (5) has not been adjudicated incompetent; (6) is not a chronic or habitual drunkard; and (7) demonstrates competence with a firearm.

There is a final note in the law, carefully worded for the benefit of those who administer it: "The licensing law shall be liberally construed to carry out the Constitutional right to bear arms for self-defense."

Pennsylvania's law is similar. The application is to be filed with the chief of police of the city of residence, or the county sheriff where the applicant resides. The license is valid for five years, and the fee is $19. The law states that "the issuing officer shall, within forty-five days, issue the license unless good cause exists to deny."

In the most comprehensive study of right-to-carry laws throughout the nation, John Lott and David Mustard, both of the University of Chicago, found that violent crime decreased dramatically in states that made it legal to carry concealed handguns. Lott and Mustard analyzed crime rates in all counties in the U.S. from 1987 to 1992. In counties that had right-to-carry laws in effect, the ratio of murder *decreased* by 8.5 percent, rape by 5 percent, and aggravated assault by 7 percent while crime rates *increased* in counties with no right-to-carry laws.

Results of the study were released August 9, 1996. The results overwhelmingly support the idea that these laws deter violent crime.

And there's a wrinkle.

The sharp drop in violent crime rates, says John Lott, isn't primarily caused by people defending themselves with guns. Rather, criminals seem to alter their behavior to avoid the possibility of coming into contact with a victim with a gun. The author concludes that guns in the hands of responsible people make all decent citizens safer, including those who don't own firearms and don't want anyone else to own one.

Since 1987, the number of states making it legal to carry firearms has increased from nine to thirty-one.

When Jim Eichelberg made the decision to carry a concealed weapon, he never dreamed that one day he would use his firearm to protect his own life. He just felt that he'd made a prudent decision, like placing an electronic burglar alarm system inside his home.

On February 19, 1997, his decision paid off.

7

Tourist Trap

"His image with the other inmates might suffer somewhat once they learn a 60-year-old woman wrestled him to the ground, took his gun away, and then he begged for his life."
—Spokesperson for the Orlando Police Department

Demetreus Jerome Lowe had an attitude. The five-foot-eight, 135-pound dude hated cops. In the three years since he turned 18, Lowe had been arrested sixteen times.

Lowe grew up near the notorious Ivey Lane projects in Orlando, Florida. His records as a juvenile are sealed, but reports indicate he was in trouble early on.

Lowe's criminal adventures as an adult began on July 5, 1994. Two deputies from the Uniform Drug Unit of the Orange County Sheriff's Department were patrolling Gore Avenue on foot. At the corner of Ivey Lane and Gore, they encountered a group of males loitering and smoking. As the deputies approached, they got a whiff of cannabis.

While frisking each suspect, a deputy spotted Lowe trying to conceal something in his hand. When asked to give it up, he refused.

It took both officers applying pressure points on his wrist before he dropped the cigarette to the ground. A Valtox test indicated that it was indeed marijuana. A further search of Lowe's person yielded several additional marijuana cigarettes and three grams of cocaine.

In what would become one of the most unusual patterns in the annals of local street crime, Lowe was charged, while the other suspects were released.

Less than a week later, on the evening of July 11, 1994, Lowe was a passenger in a 1990 GEO when an Orlando Police Department patrolman pulled the vehicle over for a minor traffic violation. The officer smelled cannabis and ordered Lowe out of the car. On the floor beneath the passenger seat, the officer spotted a roach— a small marijuana cigarette.

His experience on the streets told him that Lowe might be carrying other drugs as well, and the officer knew that shoes were a favorite hiding place of narcotics users. Lowe was asked to remove his Air Nikes. At first, the suspect began to take them off, then he shoved his heel back into the right shoe. The officer struggled with him, finally pulling the shoe from Lowe's foot. Inside, he found a white sock and a ziplock baggie with two grams of crack cocaine.

Lowe was arrested for possession of a controlled substance while the driver of the GEO was released with a traffic citation.

After several more arrests, Lowe was busted again in October 1994. This time he was sentenced to a short term in the Orange County Jail for possession of cocaine with the intent to resell it. Within a day of his release in February 1995, he was arrested for selling crack cocaine to an undercover officer for twenty dollars.

The "crack," however, was later identified as soap, and he was released when the charges were dropped.

Lowe was an angry young man, resentful of the authority represented by the police. Most times when arrested, he would resist—but without violence. And while every successful criminal attempts to remain unobtrusive, Lowe appeared to go out of his way to gain the attention of any law enforcement officer within sight. After several arrests in 1995, Lowe still had not served any meaningful jail time.

On June 26, 1996, three uniformed officers were standing near the corner of Ivey and Gore. Lowe observed them, strode up and asked, "What's up, Bro?"

The officers ignored him.

Lowe, thinking he'd been "dissed," became abusive. He began screaming obscenities at the officers.

After being told to calm down, Lowe yelled, "I don't do shit for you!"

A crowd had gathered, and a bystander whispered to Lowe, "You better cool it, Bro."

Not in the mood to heed rational advice, Lowe became even more infuriated. Bellying up to the officers, he shouted at them, like a baseball manager berating an umpire.

The onlookers began to edge away. Finally, the officers had had enough. They took Lowe down and handcuffed him.

Never one to learn from experience, Lowe's high volume of arrests increased throughout 1996 and 1997. One jailer asked him, "Have you ever thought about another line of work? Like maybe getting a real job?" As usual, Lowe disregarded the suggestion.

Hooked on crack and using marijuana when he couldn't afford cocaine, Lowe began selling drugs in earnest. However, his luck at avoiding arrest was no better than back when he was primarily a user. During 1997, he was busted time and again.

For a couple of months, Lowe peddled crack cocaine for a front man. He sold the merchandise, paid the supplier, then was given his fee. In his world, this was a typical way to support a drug habit. But, predictably, Lowe failed to pay his pusher and suddenly found himself without a steady income. And he found himself an outcast among the local drug merchants.

The only way he could procure drugs now was with a handful of cash.

• • •

The Ivey Lane projects are a long way from the glittering attractions of Disney World, Universal Studios, Epcot, and Sea World.

At approximately 6:00 P.M., on January 21, 1998, Kenneth and Mary Ellen Moring registered at the Super 8 Universal Motel on 5900 American Way, close to Orlando's main attractions. Before going to their room, they drove across the street to a Steak 'n' Ale restaurant for dinner.

Their trip had been planned on the spur of the moment. The Morings owned the Thriftway Supermarket in Indiantown, Florida. It was one of the few in the state to sell both groceries and gasoline. In fact, Exxon Oil Company was negotiating to buy the store because it wanted the gasoline outlet. Kenneth and Mary Ellen had become weary with the negotiations and wanted to relax for a few days.

At 8:06 P.M., they returned to the motel. Kenneth parked their late-model Chrysler Town and Country van in front of the door of room 123. The couple planned to turn in early, so they could visit as many attractions as possible the following day. The weather was expected to be perfect for January in Florida, sunny and in the mid-seventies.

Kenneth later recalled, "I'd unloaded all the suitcases and Mary had gone back out after some oranges. I was over by the hand basin with my back to the door. I heard someone talking. I thought my wife must have run into somebody from back home. When I turned around, there were two men standing there, one of them with a gun pointed at me."

The smaller man brandished the gun. "Gimme your cash!" he demanded.

The second man was taller and had taken a position directly in front of the door.

The small robber had the emaciated body and frenzied eyes of a hard-core crack addict. His firearm was a silver Raven .25 caliber automatic, which he waved back and forth, first menacing Kenneth, then Mary Ellen.

Kenneth wore a "belly-pack," a zippered pouch that many tourists use to carry money, car keys, and other personal belong-ings. They are convenient to use, easy to wear, and hard for pick-pockets to access.

"You better gimme your money!" the small robber repeated. His voice was cold and deadly. Kenneth Moring quickly deter-mined that the man planned to kill him and his wife.

Mary Ellen later told investigating detectives that she would have just handed over her purse, but she'd left it in the van because her hands were full of oranges and she couldn't carry it.

Kenneth slowly brought his hand down to the belly-pack. The robbers thought he planned to hand them money.

But Moring had a surprise for them. Several years before, he'd fulfilled all the requirements and received a Florida state permit to carry a concealed weapon. Because he owned several supermarkets and citrus businesses in south Florida, he always carried a gun with him.

The initial shock had worn off, and Mary Ellen thought of headlines she'd recently read. In just two years, more than a dozen tourists had been murdered in Florida. Robbers specifically targeted out-of-state visitors and foreigners because they were unfamiliar with the area. Also, those who lived long distances away were reluctant to return and testify, even if their assailants were apprehended. For armed robbers, tourists were considered easy targets.

But nothing came easy for Demetreus Lowe.

Without realizing it, he'd made two critical mistakes. His intended victims lived only a couple of hours away. The Morings would be quite willing to come back to Orlando and testify, at little inconvenience. But more important, in his wallet Kenneth Moring carried a right-to-carry permit, and in his belly-pack he carried a .38 caliber revolver.

Demetreus Lowe would soon learn why more proficient criminals selected non-Floridians as their victims of choice.

Mary Ellen Moring saw Kenneth reaching into his pouch. She knew he was going for his gun, but she also realized that Lowe could easily shoot him before he cleared the pouch.

She shouted, "Oh, no!" and lunged at Lowe.

Taken by surprise, the gunman hesitated. Mary Ellen grabbed his handgun, then wrestled him across the room. It was an instinctive reaction to protect her husband.

Kenneth quickly pulled his gun and fired at the accomplice, who was still standing near the door. As soon as the shot rang out, the tall robber bolted out of the door.

"I hit the doorjamb," Kenneth later recalled. "I missed his head by about three inches. The bullet was lying on the floor, right under the door, when it was all over with."

Kenneth turned back to his wife. As Lowe spread his legs to gain leverage in an attempt to tear away from her, Mary Ellen twisted his gun hard so that he grunted in pain. Suddenly, Lowe went down, with Mary Ellen on top of him.

That was all Kenneth needed. He stuck the gun in Lowe's face and shouted, "You drop it or I'll kill you!"

The robber's eyes registered a cold fear, and his arm went limp. He dropped the gun. Mary Ellen kicked it away, then she got up and picked up the gun.

Lowe put his hands in front of his face and began to beg.

"Don't kill me, man! Please don't shoot!"

The barrel of Ken's gun smoked as he held it in front of Lowe's face.

"Don't move or I'll shoot!"

"Mister, please don't kill me! Please, mister! Please!"

Lowe's eyes focused on the gun aimed at his forehead. He struggled to his knees and continued to beg for his life. He clasped his hands in front of him as if in prayer.

"Jesus, don't shoot . . . Please don't . . ."

Kenneth Moring was torn between anger at the man who had accosted his wife and a sense of civic responsibility. He figured that no jury in the state of Florida would convict him if he executed the assailant, but he also knew he could not commit cold-blooded murder.

As he was debating the issue, Mary Ellen looked Kenneth in the eyes, and with steel in her voice, said, "Kenneth, do *not* shoot him!"

He relaxed his finger on the trigger, pulled away, and said, "Call 911."

Kenneth noticed Lowe inching backward toward the door, and said again, "Stay still, or I'll shoot."

By now, Lowe knew his captor would not execute him. Therefore, he decided to waste no more time on the floor. He jumped to his feet and fled out the door.

He sprinted west along the corridor toward a 1984 navy blue conversion van that idled in the parking lot. Three men in the van were yelling to Lowe, "Come on, Bro. Come on."

Kenneth and Mary ran after him. As Lowe attempted to open the door, Kenneth snapped off a shot at him. The bullet exploded against the van, ripping sparks along the roof.

The vehicle screeched off, its tires smoking across the parking lot. Lowe had lost out again. The van left without him.

He sprinted after it for nearly a block, oblivious to the blaring horns of irate motorists. A small foreign car turned into the parking lot, and Lowe almost ran into it.

The last thing Kenneth and Mary Ellen Moring saw was the back of Demetreus Lowe as he disappeared into the night.

Kenneth opened the door to his own van, reached in, and grabbed his cellular telephone to dial 911.

• • •

Across the street, off-duty Orlando Police Department Sergeant Tim Davis was moonlighting at the Malibu Grand Prix when he heard a gunshot. Rushing toward the sound, he observed a male running from the Super 8 Universal Motel. The man, dressed in dark shorts and a light-colored tank top, futilely chased a blue van until both vanished in the darkness.

Davis jumped into his own car and managed to catch sight of the fleeing van. It slowed a couple of blocks away, just long enough to pick up the man who was still in hot pursuit.

Davis caught up to it at the intersection of International Drive and Kirkman Road. On a napkin, he wrote down Florida tag number XDE-58L. He then drove back to the motel, where he observed officers responding to the scene of the shooting. Davis relayed the tag number to investigating officers.

Less than thirty minutes later, Orlando police officers observed the blue conversion van speeding on King Cole Boulevard. Four suspects were in the vehicle, and the officers called for backup.

With flashing lights, they pulled it over, and detained all of the occupants.

Kenneth and Mary Ellen Moring and a witness to the attempted armed robbery, a security guard, identified Demetreus Lowe as the principal.

Lowe was arrested.

A tall man in the van resembled the second robber, but they were unable to positively identify him.

Kenneth Moring handed over Lowe's gun to investigating officers. The suspect's fingerprints were all over it.

One police officer stated to the media, "Demetreus Jerome Lowe has spent as much time in the Orange County Jail during the past three years as some of the staff who work there. Now maybe he'll spend some time at *state* expense."

In keeping with Lowe's track record, there was not probable cause to arrest the other occupants of the van.

• • •

Kenneth and Mary Ellen Moring were taken into seclusion by an Orange County Sheriff's Department tourist advocate. Arrangements were made to move them to a different hotel, and they were fed and given complimentary tickets to several local tourist attractions.

Kenneth Moring recently summed up his feelings on gun control. "We should never let the government take our guns from us," he said. "My wife saved my life, and when I got my gun out, I saved both of our lives. If I had not had it, who knows what might have happened. You can imagine the worst."

Police refused to charge Kenneth Moring, even though the robbers were fleeing when he fired the second shot. Moring, the authorities decided, was in fear of his and Mary's lives.

Demetreus Jerome Lowe sits in the Orange County Jail awaiting trial.

Ken and Mary Moring state that they will return to testify against him. If convicted, he could face up to ten years in the state prison.

Recounting the experience, Mary Ellen Moring said, "I felt the presence of God was in that room, and He protected *all* of us."

8

Rendezvous with Crackheads

"Crack makes maggots outa your brains. You'll sell out your mama, your daddy your wife, or your children for one hit."
—*Unidentified Ocala City police officer*

Every street cop in America knows that crack cocaine is the most potent drug on earth. A high percentage of violent crimes in this country are perpetrated to get money to buy the drug.

Crack cocaine, or freebase, is created by cooking powdered cocaine with baking soda. When cooled, the product is hammered into curly white flakes that resemble bits of shaved soap, or paint peelings. A flake is called a "rock."

Addiction is swift, and the prospects for recovery are bleak. Smokable cocaine doesn't trickle into the brain—it overwhelms it. The high is an intense burst of pleasure. But the downside is a free fall into a deep depression. Addicts say you rise through the ceiling, then crash back through the floor. The user, desperate to postpone the brutal collapse that follows when the dose wears off, quickly learns the strategy of obtaining, in one transaction, as many rocks as possible.

But no matter how much you have, it's never enough. A terrifying cost comes with prolonged usage—a horrible craving that makes users go berserk. It creeps into the mind minutes after the last rock is smoked up. The addict *must* get more. So he picks up whatever weapon is available and goes shopping. And that's where law-abiding citizens all too often get sucked into a crack-head's world.

• • •

It was just before dawn, November 23, 1995. The Marion County, Florida, Sheriff's Department 911 operator picked up the telephone. The receiver crackled.

"Can you get a patrol car out here?"

The voice on the other end sounded gruff, yet kindly. Like somebody's favorite uncle.

He identified himself as James Johns, 80, of Oklawaha, and gave his address. The town is near the shores of Rodman Reservoir, and backs up to the Ocala National Forest.

"What happened?"

"I just caught someone breaking in my house," Johns said calmly. "I'm holding him with my gun."

"Where is he now?"

"He's lying on the floor in my bedroom."

Johns described the intruder as a white male with long, dark hair. "His hands are behind his head. I told him if he even twitches I'll shoot him."

"Is he causing any problems?"

"No. If he causes me a problem, he won't be causing problems for anyone else."

Johns told the dispatcher he'd been robbed of a large sum of money several years earlier. He'd bought a gun to protect himself and his valuables.

Suddenly, the line went blank. The dispatcher heard the sounds of a struggle. Over the grunts of two men fighting, she heard screaming.

Then came the sharp crack of a gunshot. There was another scream, then another gunshot.

"Sir, what is going on?" the dispatcher asked, alarm ringing in her voice.

After nearly a minute of silence on the other end of the line, the dispatcher heard heavy breathing.

"I need to know what's happening," she demanded.

"All I know is he made a move, and I shot him. . . ."

The sound of sirens interrupted the transmission. The dispatcher heard Johns explaining to deputies what had happened.

Lawmen followed a trail of blood from Johns's home into a wooded area. Chadwick Fini Brown, hidden beneath a stand of palmettos, lunged at the first deputy to approach. He was quickly subdued and found to be carrying a pocketknife as well as $1,400 in cash he'd stolen from Johns.

He was also carrying a crack pipe.

Brown was taken to Munroe Regional Medical Center with a .22 caliber bullet wound between the shoulder blades. Doctors decided that the bullet would cause no permanent damage and left it in his body.

He was charged with armed burglary of an occupied dwelling, grand theft, resisting an officer with violence, possession of drug paraphernalia, and possession of an altered driver's license.

The wounded felon had numerous arrests for drugs. He'd quickly moved from a casual user of marijuana to a crack addict.

Marion County Sheriff Ken Ergle has handily won two elections on a get-tough-on-criminals platform. After the incident, he stated, "All homes should have a gun in them so the homeowner can protect himself and his family. . . . I'm telling you, if somebody broke into my house while me and my family were in there, I would be in fear of my life. And I would do everything in my power to eliminate that fear or threat."

Brown's father disagreed. "That was not a justified shooting," he said. "It has to be life-threatening, and life-threatening is a situation where a man has a knife on you, or a gun or something. [My son] was trying to get out a window."

A few days later, the case was brought to the state attorney's Office. The shooting was ruled justifiable. No charges were brought against Johns.

"If you read the [Florida state] statute," an officer said, "it says if someone commits a felony while in your house, you can shoot him."

On January 23, the *Ocala Star Banner* conducted a poll of its readers, asking if they would shoot an intruder if he broke into their homes. The majority—97.5 percent—said they would; 2.5 percent said they would not. "If he comes through the window," said one reader, "he goes out in a box."

On November 23, 1995, Chadwick Fini Brown learned that

crack cocaine is not worth the cost. But at least he's alive to ponder the lesson. Many other users who turn to crime are not so lucky.

• • •

J. Edwin "Mac" MacDonald, 73, slept with a pistol under his pillow. In 1984, two men broke into his home and robbed him of $5,000 in cash. He promised himself then that it wouldn't happen again.

He lived in a small trailer near Williston, Florida. He'd trained horses for most of his life and still kept a few Paso Finas on his ranch. He loved to get up early and see their breath smoking in the early morning chill.

At midnight on January 27, 1996, MacDonald awoke.

By the light of a nearby street lamp, he saw a shadow moving about the room.

A flashback momentarily paralyzed him: two strangers holding a shotgun to his head. Fear exploded in him like gunpowder.

He rubbed his eyes to adjust to the darkness. Someone stood over him.

MacDonald fished for the .22 caliber revolver beneath his pillow.

"Gimme some money!"

The voice sounded strangely disconnected from reality.

By now, MacDonald's eyes were adjusting to the darkness. He saw a thin male with long, curly hair. The intruder wore a faded red T-shirt, black jeans, and black wool gloves.

The man turned away and began to pull at the chest of drawers. He jerked out a drawer and dumped the contents on the floor.

"Where do you keep your money?" he demanded.

MacDonald had had enough. He jumped from his bed, straightened up, and pointed his pistol at the intruder.

"Get out of here!"

The man hesitated, then darted from the room.

The homeowner breathed a sigh of relief. He planned to walk to the telephone in the living room and call the police. But before he could move, he heard footsteps in the kitchen. The man had not left.

MacDonald stepped to the door of the bedroom.

The intruder appeared before him, holding a lamp. MacDonald pointed his gun at the man.

"Get the hell outa here!" he repeated.

The intruder flung the lamp at MacDonald. It shattered against the wall. He then lunged at the home owner. The old man aimed his gun at the ceiling, but when he fired, the man didn't flee.

Instead he just laughed.

"You're shooting blanks," he said. From his belt, he pulled a skinning knife and held it up to the light.

His laughter was eerie, MacDonald thought. Probably high on drugs, the old-timer concluded.

MacDonald began to backpedal into the bedroom. The man swung the knife back and forth, his eyes menacing MacDonald. He slashed at him with the blade. The home owner felt warm blood trickling from a gash in his arm.

"I'll shoot!"

The intruder rushed him, and MacDonald aimed at his chest and pulled the trigger.

This time the assailant gasped, turned, and stumbled out of the room.

MacDonald rushed past him, pushing the assailant to the floor. But the man scrambled to his feet and ran from the house. The home owner turned on the lights, then went to the telephone to call police. But when he picked it up, there was only silence. He walked out the door and found the intruder lying on the ground, moaning.

MacDonald jumped into his car and made the five-minute drive to Williston to report the shooting. The small town lies in rural Levy County, twenty-five miles west of Ocala.

At 12:56 A.M., his car squealed into the driveway of the Williston Police Department. Sergeant Clay Connolly met the distraught man. As a paramedic bandaged his bloody arm, MacDonald recounted the incident to the officer. When Connolly asked what had happened to the intruder, MacDonald simply said, "I shot him."

Connolly asked the dispatcher to call the Marion County Sheriff's Department and have them meet him at the scene. MacDonald lived just inside the Marion County line, and the sergeant didn't want any jurisdictional disputes.

At 1:20 A.M., Connolly found the horse trainer's house and pulled into the front yard. His headlights focused on a white male lying face down on the ground. Connolly got out, checked for a pulse, and found none. He then rolled the man on his back and shined his flashlight into his eyes. The pupils didn't react to the light.

The Marion County Sheriff's Department still had not arrived, so Connolly conducted a preliminary investigation. The window of the front door had been broken, and a screen curtain was pulled back. From the door, he shone his flashlight into the hallway, and saw what had been a table lamp. Now it was just shattered pieces of glass.

At this time, a Marion County sheriff's deputy drove up. He and Connolly took a closer look at the corpse. They saw two puncture wounds in the upper chest. But there was very little bleeding.

A billfold discovered on the man identified him as 20-year-old Jonathan Hardy Silas.

Further investigation revealed that Silas had been smoking crack cocaine with friends and had run out of drugs. Desperate for more, the friends drove Silas to the trailer because it looked like an easy target. While Silas burglarized the place, his friends sat in the car and waited. When they saw Silas run out of the house and collapse on the lawn, they panicked and sped away. Crackheads don't retrieve their dead and wounded.

Silas was also the chief suspect in another home invasion two nights earlier.

On March 28, 1996, a grand jury refused to indict MacDonald.

The horse trainer was puzzled about how the first shot hit the suspect. He had aimed "high." Detectives speculated that the gun must have fired early, hitting Silas in the chest on the way up.

"It's very disturbing," MacDonald said. "It's something you can't explain to nobody. It's a feeling I'll probably carry the rest of my life.

"He was just a young boy. But when they come at you with a knife, it's a little bit hard to look the other way. He had all the opportunity to leave. There was nothing I could do except what I did."

• • •

On the afternoon of Saturday, November 24, 1990, Brian Rigsby left his home outside Atlanta, Georgia, after saying good-bye to his wife. He picked up his friend Tom Styer for a hastily arranged camping trip.

Getting a late start, and making a few wrong turns in the Oconee National Forest, the two friends didn't arrive at their campsites until well after dark. They chose a spot near the public rifle range and looked forward to some target-shooting the next day.

By the light of a lantern, the friends pitched a tent and built a campfire. They were settling in for the night when they heard the distinctive growl of a diesel engine approaching. Shortly thereafter, a truck pulled up in the middle of their camp. The name of a local business was stenciled on the side.

Two men got out and introduced themselves. They were driving around, they explained, to seek out visitors and help them with their chores. Overly polite, the two men insisted on helping Rigsby and Styer cut more firewood. During their hour-long stay, the courteous twosome said they were long-time residents of the area. They also boasted about their extensive knowledge of the surrounding woods and their prowess as hunters.

Rigsby remembers feeling uncomfortable with the two men. They talked fast but couldn't seem to focus on what they were saying. He was relieved when they finally left. He and Styer discussed moving to another location to avoid the men, but finally decided to retire for the night.

A few minutes later, they heard the truck's diesel engine coming back down the road to their camp.

The truck pulled up short, and its engine abruptly cut off. In the quiet that followed, Rigsby and Styer heard the faint crackle of leaves rustling.

Each camper grabbed his gun and made sure it was loaded. Rigsby took cover behind his truck, armed with a Ruger Mini-14 with a thirty-round magazine. Styer knelt in the tent's shadow with his .45 pistol at the ready.

"I tried to listen for the men," Rigsby recalled. "But I couldn't hear much over the sound of my breathing. Except the pounding of my heart."

It was Styer who saw them first. One of the men stepped suddenly into the light cast by the campfire. Then he raised a double-barrel shotgun and aimed it in Rigsby's direction. Rigsby kept his head down. He heard Styer ask the man why they'd come back.

"Because I'm going to kill you," he replied, and swung his shotgun around at Styer.

Styer instructed the aggressor to drop his gun.

Instead, he fired.

Rigsby heard Styer scream in agony.

Rigsby remembers seeing the front sight of his Mini-14 centered on the assailant's chest. He fired twice. Then he swung the rifle to where he thought the second gunman should be. Rigsby cranked off six more rounds, using as a target the flash from his adversary's muzzle against the blackness of the surrounding forest.

Partially blinded by the blaze from his own weapon, Rigsby dropped back down behind his truck. He looked from underneath the frame, scanning the campsite. Seeing no one, he yelled for Styer. There was no answer.

He called out again, but heard no response.

Rigsby knew that the first attacker was down and no longer posed a threat. But the other gunman was out there. Somewhere.

After waiting a few minutes, he called again to Styer. But his friend still didn't answer.

Rigsby began to move backward, slowly and cautiously, away from the camp. Seeing a light through the trees, he started toward it. Amazingly, it was a camp full of hunters. After he told them what had happened, one rushed to find a telephone.

The police responded quickly and handcuffed Rigsby as a material witness pending the outcome of the investigation. Then he and the officers returned to the scene of the attack.

They found Styer, seriously wounded but still alive.

The shotgun-wielding assailant had been hit twice and died instantly. His accomplice had also taken two rounds but would survive. Both men had carried twelve-gauge shotguns loaded with three-inch Magnum buckshot. And both men had fired their weapons at the two campers.

The two friends gave statements to the police, whereupon Rigsby was released from custody. Styer was rushed to a local hospital to have buckshot removed from both legs.

In his statement, the surviving gunman admitted he and his partner had returned to rob the campers. They'd hatched their plan while smoking crack cocaine following the first visit to the campsite.

Later, an officer told Rigsby and Styer that their attackers would have murdered both men. When introducing themselves, they gave their real names, and they drove a truck owned by their employer. Apparently, in their crack-induced haze, they hadn't intended to leave any witnesses.

• • •

Crack cocaine can precipitate great human tragedies. It can also produce comedy of the basest sort.

The day before the 4th of July, 1995, had been one of those hot, sweaty days that keep most people indoors. Near Summerfield, Florida, in rural Marion County, David Perry Johnson was on the make for crack cocaine. Just one rock, he thought. Anything for one more high.

On his way to work, Harold Scott, 36, was parked at the Summerfield Country Store in the early morning. Johnson, 30, opened the door of Scott's 1987 Pontiac Grand Am and climbed in. He told the driver he would kill him if he didn't drive to Ocala, about fifteen miles away.

Although Scott never saw a weapon, Johnson stated he had a gun in his pocket.

Scott drove north toward Ocala. They came to another convenience store, and Johnson ordered Scott to stop. Johnson said he planned to rob the store and demanded that Scott park the car and wait on him. The driver, however, decided that he would speed off and call the police as soon as Johnson left the car.

Johnson may have sensed Scott's intentions, because instead of getting out of the car, he ordered Scott to continue driving north.

Finally, he told Scott to drive to Marion Community Hospital in

Ocala. In the parking lot, Johnson spotted a Tom's snack delivery truck. Johnson jumped from the car and rushed up to the truck. Scott immediately drove away, found a telephone, and called police.

The driver of the delivery truck, James Irizarry, 45, was inside the back of the truck when the door opened. Johnson pushed himself into the truck and ordered the driver, "Give me some chips."

Irizarry was taken by surprise but quickly recovered. He carried a .25 caliber handgun and reached into his pocket for it.

Johnson, thinking he was reaching for money, said, "Give me some cash, too."

Instead of cash, Irizarry pulled out the .25. The two men struggled for the weapon before the truck driver pushed Johnson away. As Irizarry aimed the gun at him, Johnson dived from the truck.

He rushed to where he'd left Scott and found him gone. He began cursing the driver of the car, then remembered that the Tom's truck driver had a gun.

Johnson raced from the scene, crossed Pine Street, and ran to a house on Southwest 15th Street.

Lee Breeding, the home owner, later recalled, "I heard him when he went under the floor [of the house]. He had to pull a lawn mower out and that made me suspicious. Then I saw the police riding around shining their spotlights, and that got me more suspicious. I went out there and shined my flashlight, and there he was. . . . I had protection. I wasn't going out there with a flashlight and not have some protection in my other hand."

Johnson was arrested and booked into the Marion County Jail on one count each of attempted strong-arm robbery, burglary of an occupied automobile, and false imprisonment.

David Perry Johnson was so strung out on crack cocaine that he gave police a false name, lay down on the floor, and proceeded to go into a deep sleep.

Ocala Police Department investigators weren't surprised that a crack cocaine addict would risk ten years in jail for trying to steal a bag of potato chips.

One veteran investigator said, "A bag of chips? He probably thought he could trade them for a rock."

9

Death of a Serial Killer

Your injury has no healing, your wound is severe. All who
hear news of you will clap their hands over you, for upon
whom has not your wickedness passed continually?
—Nahum 3:19 (NKJV)

Five-year-old Siobhan McGuinness was the first to die.
Abducted from the streets of Missoula, Montana, on
February 5, 1974, her body was found the next afternoon. She
had been sexually assaulted, beaten, and stabbed. According to the
medical examiner, it had taken her from eight to twelve hours to
die of her wounds. In fact, a blood trail through the snow indicated that she was still alive when dumped along a roadside.
Evidence suggested that the child had tried to crawl from a culvert
to the bank of the road before dying. It was a brutal, shocking
murder in what was normally a peaceful western town.

But it was only the first.

Donna Pounds was next. On April 11, 1974, the minister's wife
was attacked in her own home, tied to her bed with white clothesline, and raped. Then she was released and led to the basement,

where she was shot execution-style. The murderer left the gun pushed up into her vagina.

In September 1985, the decomposed skeleton of an unidentified female was discovered buried on a mountain above Missoula. Two other skeletons had been found in the area, one identified as Devonna Nelson, a 15-year-old hitchhiker from Seattle, Washington. The third skeleton remained unidentified. Each had been shot at close range with a .22 caliber handgun.

● ● ●

On December 13, 1985, twelve days before Christmas, Mike and Teresa Shook, and their children, Matt, Luke, and Megan, got ready for bed. The family had spent a pleasant evening in their new home decorating the Christmas tree. Without warning, a man burst through the door holding a .22 Ruger. He quickly subdued Mike, tying him up, then stabbing him in the chest. As the life drained from him, Mike saw the intruder shoot Teresa in the ankle, then carry her screaming and struggling to the bedroom. He tied her to the bedposts with white clothesline and raped her as 2½-year-old Megan watched from her crib. After ravaging Teresa, the intruder unsuccessfully attempted to cut the bullet from her ankle. Finally, he put her out of her misery, stabbing her to death.

As the children hid in their bedrooms, the murderer spent the night inside the house. Just before dawn, he stole a few items, set fire to a sofa, and left. Fortunately for the Shook children, whom the intruder locked inside the house, the fire didn't take. The three

DEATH OF A SERIAL KILLER   133

children survived, but the fumes and gases from the smoldering flames almost killed them.

A few days after that brutal double-murder, Kris Wells, the slim, attractive, 33-year-old manager of Conlin's Furniture Company, had to reprimand one of her delivery men. Wayne Nance, a muscular, red-haired barroom bouncer, had become increasingly insolent toward her and his coworkers. He had begun to draw weird pictures and symbols on the furniture boxes—satanic symbols such as crosses and skulls. Had she known that he had drilled a peephole through one of the walls so that he could see into the ladies' restroom, she would have had no choice but to fire him.

As she spoke to Nance, Wells didn't know that the delivery man suffered from a psychosis that had led him to commit at least ten murders. And she didn't know that Nance was stalking her, was obsessed with her, and would only be satisfied when he possessed her.

Kristen Zimmerman Wells was born in Illinois. After earning a bachelor's degree in interior design from the University of Iowa, she married Doug Wells and moved to Missoula, Montana. Kris obtained a job with Conlin's Furniture Company, beginning as sales manager. Diligent and talented, she quickly worked her way up to store manager.

Doug, her husband, owned Lock, Stock & Barrel, a gunsmith shop. He kept in shape by hunting, fishing, and hiking in the nearby mountains. Kris and Doug lived a simple life, enjoying Saturday afternoon football games, visiting with friends, barbecuing steaks after work, and occasionally going out to restaurants for dinner.

Kris jogged the country roads near her home, unaware that Wayne Nance was hidden nearby with his ever-present camera, taking pictures that he would later enlarge and keep in a treasured cardboard box. He fantasized about Kris while cutting samples of her writing from work orders at the store—then he would clip and paste the words beneath the pictures so that they said things such as, "I love you, Wayne." At night he would park for hours outside her house, watching, dreaming, fantasizing. This silent stalking went on for months.

The evening of September 2, 1986, was cool, but the hard freeze of winter had not yet set in. Kris and Doug returned home after an evening at a local shooting range, followed by dinner with friends. Both were tired, and while Kris prepared for bed, Doug did a couple of chores. He first placed the gun he'd used at the range, an antique lever-action Savage Model 99G Take-Down, near his workbench in the basement. He also placed a box of homemade cartridges on the bench. Then he went through the garage to take out the trash.

As he moved into the yard, he noticed a movement behind a bush. His mouth jerked open, and he snapped, "Who's there?"

"Wayne from Conlin's."

"What the hell are you doing here?" Doug asked.

Nance stuttered for a moment, then said that he'd seen something suspicious. He asked Doug to get his flashlight. In the moment that Doug turned to comply, he knew he'd made a mistake.

But it was too late.

Doug felt a searing shock to the back of his head, and a burst of white light exploded in his skull. He fell, almost unconscious, his eyes blurry. Blood spurted out of a deep wound in his scalp.

When he looked up, Wayne was standing over him holding a lead pipe wrapped with tape. Doug pulled away, trying to back up and kick Wayne at the same time.

Doug had met Wayne Nance a few times, but had never seen him as intense and seething with rage as he was now. As Wayne approached, Doug kicked him and they fell together, struggling and grunting as they fought. They rolled through the garage, back toward the steps, and thumped back into the house. In the living room, Doug held on as his assailant rained blows on him with the club.

Kris heard the struggle and raced from the bedroom to see what was causing the commotion. The color drained from her face when she saw her husband engaged in a death struggle with an intruder.

As she started toward them, Wayne broke away from Doug and pulled a .22 Ruger revolver from a pouch he wore on his belt. Kris was dressed only in her white nightgown, and Wayne, pointing the gun at Doug, leered at her.

He screamed, "I've got a gun!" This fact was brutally obvious to the fearful home owners.

Kris moved over to Doug, took his head in her hands, and attempted to stop the bleeding. She shouted for Wayne to leave, but he stood, waving the gun and boiling with fury. Finally, he yelled, "Get away. Give me room."

Kris and Doug backed away together, Doug on his buttocks like a crab scuttling across the floor, while Kris continued to hold his head. It was an eerie dance of desperation that drove them all the way to the living room wall.

Wayne began to mumble, stating that he'd done something bad and needed money to get out of town. Kris told him where the company receipts were located and gave him her pocketbook, hoping he would take the money and leave. Instead, he pulled a roll of white clothesline from his pouch. Using a kitchen knife that he carried in a sheath on his belt, he cut the rope into sections.

Doug was drifting in and out, but managed to remain conscious despite the blood gushing from his head. Kris begged Wayne not to tie them, but he was acting freaky. He paced back and forth, talking to himself. Finally, he moved across the room and tied Doug. At her request, he brought Kris a towel so she could stop Doug's bleeding.

After nearly a half hour, Wayne took Kris to the bedroom, and laid her across the bed. There he used the ropes to tie her hands and feet to the frame. She was vulnerable and very frightened. Kris noticed that Wayne had purposely loosened the rope on her left arm. The reason had to be sinister, she thought, and her sudden realization of the depth of his psychosis drove a sickening fear into her.

After tying Kris, Wayne went to the chest of drawers and removed a white athletic sock and a pair of pantyhose. He stuffed the sock into her mouth and tied the hose around her head to hold it so that she couldn't talk.

During the time he'd been in their house, Wayne had seemed unpredictable, pacing back and forth, as if he had no plan. His actions kept Kris and Doug on edge. Is he dangerous? the couple wondered. Is he going to kill us? What's his purpose here?

He would talk to himself as if they weren't in the room, sometimes asking questions, and then answering them. His actions were bizarre, and both Doug and Kris realized that if they made a wrong move they would be dead.

After tying Kris to the bed, Wayne returned to the living room, pulled Doug to his feet, and guided him down the stairs to the basement. A supporting beam stood in the center of the floor, beside the workbench, and Wayne pushed Doug against the post. Doug's hands were still tied behind his back, and he was weak from losing a massive quantity of blood. As Doug collapsed against the post, Wayne suddenly began to punch him in the face. Doug twisted away, but immediately stopped when he saw the gun trained on him.

"Get back against that post or I'll shoot you." Wayne's voice chopped into Doug like a hatchet.

Wayne pulled additional clothesline from his pouch and began to tie Doug to the post. He started by wrapping the rope around Doug's neck and tying it to the post. Then he tied his shoulders and feet.

Immediately after securing Doug, Wayne began a series of wild comings and goings, banging the door of the basement shut and running up to check Kris, then racing back down the stairs to check Doug.

Doug knew the Savage was on the workbench, just out of his reach. If he could break free, they would have a chance. Through the pain and the blurred vision, he tugged at the ropes, trying to free himself.

Wayne came back into the basement, mumbling to himself. His soliloquy frightened Doug. Wayne jerked away again, and Doug heard him racing up the stairs.

In the bedroom, Kris was struggling against the ropes. She'd gotten her left arm free, but when she heard Wayne coming she replaced the ropes as if she were tied. Wayne looked in on her, then raced back down the stairs.

This time he didn't hesitate. He walked behind Doug and suddenly plunged an oak-handled knife into Doug's chest. The blade punctured a lung, sliced through the diaphragm, and stopped a fraction of an inch short of his heart.

Doug almost fainted from the pain. He heard air bubbling in his chest. The room faded, as if he were moving slowly away from his own existence. He *had* to remain conscious, to suck the life back into his body, to keep it from draining away.

Then Wayne moved around in front of Doug and jerked the knife out of his chest. As Doug watched with glazed, smoky eyes, Wayne smiled. He began to wipe blood from the blade with the cuff of Doug's pants.

Doug collapsed, held up only by the ropes. His will could keep him alive for only so long.

Wayne stood. He was purposeful now when he left. This time he didn't even bother to slam the door shut.

When Wayne reentered the bedroom, he saw that Kris was almost free. She had worked her left hand loose, and then untied her feet. Given a few more seconds, she would have freed herself completely. She had planned to dive through the window and run to her neighbor's house for help.

"You called the cops, didn't you?" Wayne asked, pulling the sock out of her mouth.

"No. You'd have heard me."

He began to retie Kris.

In the basement, Doug wouldn't die. He'd gained new

adrenaline and began to struggle. Twisting his head beneath the rope so that it fell away, he pulled free of the clothesline tied around his shoulders. Finally, he tugged out of the ropes that bound his hands and feet.

Doug knew that this was his last chance. He stood and lurched toward the workbench. Blood drained from his head and chest as he picked up the rifle and snapped a shell into the chamber.

Doug didn't want to confront Wayne in the bedroom, where the intruder could use Kris as a shield. Plus, he didn't know if he could even make it to the bedroom. In his bloody haze, he realized that Wayne would run back down to the basement if he heard a noise.

Doug slapped the butt of the rifle against the wall. Sure enough, as soon as he heard the sound, Wayne rushed from the bedroom. Doug could hear his footsteps tapping across the floor toward the stairs that led to the basement.

He knew he had one shot.

As soon as Wayne crossed into view, illuminated by a light, Doug fired. The explosion rocked the small basement, and smoke from the antique gun whispered into the air. Wayne scampered away, out of sight.

Doug thought he'd missed. Then he heard Wayne fall.

The intruder began to kick the floor. The reverberations sounded like gunshots, and Doug tensed.

Then he heard Wayne wail, "*Oh my God! I'm a dead man!*"

Hearing the shot, Kris thought that Wayne had killed Doug, and she knew it was only a matter of seconds before she would be raped and murdered. She began to claw desperately at the ropes.

Finally, she was free, except for her right hand.

Doug staggered up the stairs and saw Wayne trying to rise. Doug grasped the rifle by its barrel and swung with all the might he could muster. He caught Wayne squarely on the head, knocking him back down. Then, with a fury and rage that he had never known, Doug began to pound at Wayne. The intruder scooted along the floor toward the bedroom as Doug repeatedly slammed him with the butt of the rifle.

The medical examiner later concluded that Doug had hit Wayne sixty times in an attack that lasted barely a minute. One blow every second, triggered by desperation.

At the bedroom door, the stock of the rifle splintered. Wayne begged Doug to stop hitting him, but Doug continued swinging the remaining part of the gun, until Wayne had crawled as far as he could into the bedroom. He'd been beaten into the space between the bed and the nightstand.

Kris, with her right hand still tied to the bed, began punching and kicking at Wayne.

Wayne reached into his pouch, and pulled his own gun. The concussion of the shot shook the little bedroom, but the bullet whistled harmlessly into the ceiling. The shot only added to the intensity of the couple's attack on Wayne.

Doug continued to bring the gun barrel down on Wayne, again and again.

Wayne pushed his gun toward Doug; the explosion made Doug's leg go numb. The bullet had struck him above the knee, but the pain made him fight harder. He swung the barrel of the rifle again, shattering the lamp on the nightstand, and pitching the room into darkness.

By now the struggle had gone on for more than a minute.

Suddenly, another explosion flashed in the darkness. Doug remembered that he kept an automatic in the nightstand, and lunged across the room to get it. In the same motion he flipped on the overhead light.

He aimed at Wayne, prepared to send six bullets into the intruder. But Wayne was slumped on the floor, twitching, convulsing, moaning. Doug instinctively knew that Wayne had shot himself. The Ruger was grasped in a death-grip, pointed at Wayne's ear.

During the struggle, Kris had finally freed herself. She was literally shell-shocked but was able to pull the gun from Wayne's hand.

Doug collapsed onto the bed as Kris rushed to call 911.

● ● ●

Wayne Nance died a few hours later.

The bullet from Doug's rifle had passed through his body and severed the renal artery, the spleen, the pancreas, and the right lung. He had also suffered numerous bruises and lacerations from the stock and barrel of Doug's rifle.

Doug, semiconscious, was transported to the hospital where it was determined that the knife had sliced his diaphragm and punctured a lung. It took twenty-two stitches to sew up the gash on his head. For two years, he had to walk with a leg brace because the bullet had hit the sciatic nerve. Eventually, surgery repaired it.

The community responded with an outpouring of support. Doctors and the hospital refused to charge Doug for their services.

He received a reward from the Siobhan McGuinness Missoula Reward Fund.

Kris was not physically injured, but suffered nightmares for years afterward.

• • •

Detectives searched Wayne's house that night, finding evidence linking him to ten murders. Trophies such as earrings, weapons, and small household items stolen from many of his victims were found, as well as photographs of many of them. Bullets from his gun matched the bullets found in several victims, including the one found in Teresa Shook's ankle and the bodies of the women found on the mountains above Missoula.

Wayne Nance is suspected in several other unsolved slayings that occurred in counties surrounding Missoula between 1974 and 1986.

In the last few years, Doug and Kris Wells have become regular lecturers at the FBI Behavioral Sciences Unit in Quantico, Virginia. This unit, developed to learn more about multiple murders, is the world's leading authority on serial killers. Because Doug and Kris are among the few individuals known to have successfully fought off a serial killer, the unit felt that their trainees could gain first-hand knowledge of how a serial killer acts during the commission of his crimes.

FBI agents feel that Wayne Nance typified the organized serial killer. He began with Siobhan McGuinness, an "easy" kill. After tasting blood, Nance gravitated to what he considered slightly more difficult victims—women who were alone. Finally, the ultimate thrill was to capture a husband and wife together, kill the husband as the wife watched, then ravage and kill the wife. That is exactly what had happened in the case of Mike and Teresa Shook.

This was also the plan for Doug and Kris Wells. To make the game sweeter, several FBI agents feel that Wayne purposely left one of Kris's ropes loose, hoping she would reject her husband, free herself, and come to Wayne. That, according to some who are familiar with the case, was Wayne's ultimate fantasy.

John Douglas, the creator of the FBI's criminal profile system, and on whom the book and movie *The Silence of the Lambs* was based, states in his book, *Mind Hunter*, that Nance's case shows that serial killers can operate successfully in small, rural communities as long as they vary their method of killing and use different jurisdictions to confuse law enforcement officials.

Since the attack, the Wellses have turned their home into a mini-fortress, arming it to the hilt and training themselves in measures to take in case of another attack.

10

Death of a Drifter

*"I'm happy. I mean I'd like to live a life of luxury and travel,
but I'm happy. I've got a whole life to live unless somebody
takes it away."*
—Rick Amoedo, July 20, 1996

On December 28, 1994, Rick Amoedo was about to close his shop. At five o'clock, his wife, Debbie, picked up their 12-year-old son, Michael, who had worked with Rick most of the day. A few minutes later, Sam Camacho, Rick's friend and part-time employee, also left to go home.

Amoedo's shop, Unique Automotive, sits on a corner lot at 800 Central Boulevard. It is typical of the other businesses in the area. Bars and fences provide a degree of protection, and as an added precaution, the front door is kept locked. Customers have to knock and undergo a physical inspection before they're allowed to enter. The shop specializes in the repair of starters and alternators, but Amoedo also contracts for general automobile repair when he has the time.

Central Boulevard in downtown Orlando, Florida, is only a few miles from Walt Disney World. It is a mean street, however, far removed from the tourist industry. At certain times of the day, hundreds of vagrants, freeloaders, and homeless people congregate at the various "soup kitchens" that have sprung up in the area. All are down on their luck—some are alcoholics, most are drug addicts, and many have histories of mental illness. A few are dangerous.

When he was 8 years old, after the Merielito riots in 1969, Ricardo Amoedo had immigrated with his parents from Cuba to Miami. One of the strongest memories he has of his early childhood is a perverted lesson his teachers tried to indoctrinate in him. On a wall in the school cafeteria, the Fidel regime had placed a picture of Jesus Christ side by side with a photograph of Fidel Castro. After lunch, teachers instructed the students to pray to Jesus for ice cream. The children all dutifully bowed and prayed. No ice cream appeared. Then they were told to pray to Castro for ice cream. After doing so, cafeteria workers appeared with bowls for everyone. "Now who do you believe in?" they were asked.

Shortly after that experience, Ricardo's parents fled Cuba for the United States. Rick lived first in Miami, then California, and finally Chicago, before moving to Orlando where his father had bought an auto repair shop. After serving four years in the Marine Corps, Amoedo came back to Orlando, married, and became a father. Soon his father died, and Rick took over the business.

In his office, a long wooden bench was cluttered with the tools and equipment needed for his occupation. An air hose dropped from the ceiling to the bench. Wire grocery baskets containing the repaired starters and alternators sat on the floor beside the bench. A metal desk held a portable telephone, an adding machine, and

Rick Amoedo, owner of Unique Automotive (below), was the intended victim of a crazed drifter who attacked him with a jackhammer at his place of business late one December evening in 1994.

assorted bills and receipts. On one wall, an air conditioner chugged, working hard to cool the place.

On that late December evening, Amoedo began walking from the office to the garage. The garage door at the rear of the building was still up, and he needed to pull it down and lock up before going home. As he entered the garage, Amoedo's head exploded. White-hot flashes, like gunfire, crashed in his brain. For a moment, he thought the roof was caving in and that he was being buried alive by the falling beams.

The shock thrust him to his knees. Amoedo's ears rang, and he felt another blow jolt him. At this point he realized he was being attacked.

Looking up, he saw a large man raise a handheld jackhammer above his head to hit him again. Auto workers called it an air chisel. Amoedo had been using it earlier to break rusty bolts on an old automobile. It was made of steel and looked similar to a drill— but more streamlined. The air chisel weighed at least twenty hard-steel pounds.

Amoedo glanced at the intruder's face to try to identify him. He'd never seen the man.

As the attacker held his weapon in the air, preparing to smash it down again, Amoedo saw it silhouetted against the lights. It was smeared with his own blood.

The intruder had evidently scaled the fence behind the garage where cars awaiting repairs were kept. Somehow, he'd sneaked in through the open door of the garage. There he'd hidden, waiting until everyone left except Amoedo. The man never said a word, but his face carried a wide-eyed, spaced-out expression. The eyes chilled Amoedo—they were glazed by drugs or sheer insanity. He wasn't sure which.

The surprise of the attack had vanished, and the ex-marine now realized that he was fighting for his life.

"*Are you crazy, man?*" he yelled, but the attacker did not answer.

Amoedo grabbed his assailant's arm and deflected the next blow. He clamped both hands around the man's wrist, trying to hold the air chisel at a distance so that it would not explode against his skull again. For a moment, the two twisted like dancers across the floor of the garage, Amoedo holding his attacker's wrist with the desperation of a drowning man.

The man seemed to have superhuman strength and continued to try to plunge the air chisel down on Amoedo. Blood streamed from Amoedo's head, soaking his shirt and pants before spreading like oil across the floor. He would eventually require forty staples to close the wounds. To Amoedo it felt as if his skull had been smashed open.

As he strained to neutralize the attack, he thought of his family. He was glad his son, Michael James, had left a few minutes earlier. He thought of his daughter, Aimee. His office was decorated with dozens of her stick drawings—they always made him smile when he saw them. His wife, Debbie, was eight months pregnant, and the thought that he might never see his unborn child gave him strength.

Amoedo wobbled to his feet and pulled the intruder's arms down to his sides, wrapping them against his body. The attacker lost his balance, and the two men tumbled to the floor. Amoedo landed on top of the man and managed to get both hands around his neck. He squeezed as hard as he could, pushing all his strength into it. His palms were bloody, and he couldn't get a good grip, but he tried to crush the man's neck with his fingers.

In a moment, he heard the man begin to gasp, as if he were trying to suck breath into constricted lungs. By now Amoedo was totally exhausted. His mind began to float away. He felt like a boxer falling from a delayed-reaction punch. He thought again of his family somewhere far away, in some netherworld that existed beyond his reach. At least they were safe.

Then he passed out.

• • •

When he opened his eyes, the intruder had vanished.

Amoedo crawled on his knees, using an automobile to pull himself to his feet, and lurched back toward his office.

At last, he thought, it's over.

He fumbled in the drawer of the desk where he kept his Taurus .357 Magnum. He yanked it from the zippered leather pouch in which he kept it stored and moved cautiously back into the garage. As he passed through the blood-smeared strips of plastic that served as a door to his office, he half expected another attack.

In the middle of the garage floor, there was a bloody pool. Several tool cases had been knocked down and tools spilled out across the floor. He kicked a wrench as he moved back into the garage.

For a moment, Amoedo breathed a sigh of relief. No one was there. It was over.

Then, from the corner of his eye, he saw a shadow plunging toward him. It was the intruder, wild-eyed and rushing him again.

"Are you crazy, man?" Amoedo repeated, but the words seemed to stick on his tongue and ended in an unintelligible scream.

He held the gun with both hands, pointing it at the charging man. He didn't even have time to drop to the shooter's stance. Almost as if the gun had a mind of its own, yellow streaks burst from it, followed by four rockets of explosions.

He heard the intruder gasp, and saw him fall. It was over in seconds. Amoedo stood in disbelief. He lowered the smoking gun and noticed he was choking for breath.

He was unable to look at the man who lay motionless on the floor. A question kept coming to him. Why? Why had he been attacked?

The sudden thought that he might go to jail for killing someone suddenly chilled him. A person that he didn't even know had ruined the life he'd worked so many years to build.

He thought again of his wife and children, the ones who meant the most to him. Conflicting emotions swept through his mind. He remembered when he'd been robbed a year before by three masked intruders, how they'd held a pistol to his temple, how the barrel had seemed as large as a shotgun, and how he'd vowed never to let it happen again.

Amoedo finally realized he needed to get help. He staggered back to the office and picked up the telephone. Between ragged breaths, he whispered into the receiver, "Somebody's dead . . . I'm dying . . . head split open . . ."

He dropped the telephone and crawled back into the garage.

At least, he must have crawled back into the garage, because the next thing he remembered was blue lights spinning off the chalk-yellow walls of the soup kitchen next door. He was lying beneath the garage door, and the intruder was nowhere to be seen. A puddle of blood stained the center of the garage floor, however, and a smear of blood showed where the intruder had fallen, gotten up, and dragged himself out into the yard.

A voice from a megaphone yelled, "Put the gun down."

Amoedo looked down at his hands and realized he was still holding the pistol. Slowly, and dramatically, he dropped it to the floor.

Voices drifted in and out. Sirens wailed, and the tires of dozens of police cars screeched to a halt along the road next to his shop. Someone yelled for him to open the front door. Because of the wire fence and the bars on the windows and the locked front door, the police were unable to enter.

Amoedo reached for his key, trying to stand and go to the door.

"Keep your hands out of your pockets!" the man with the megaphone yelled.

What the hell do these people want? It seemed that everything he did was wrong.

Finally, a police officer vaulted the fence and raced to his aid. Amoedo pushed himself into a sitting position and gasped out his story.

One of the cops followed the bloody trail across the yard to the fence. Beneath a car, they found the body of Amoedo's attacker. He'd been shot three times, twice in the chest, once in the neck. The strange thing was that only the wound to the neck had bled.

Attendants wrapped Amoedo's head, and an ambulance rushed him to Orange Regional Medical Center. In the emergency room, all he could think of was his need for water. He was so thirsty he had to have something to drink. The doctors told him he couldn't ingest liquids until after surgery, but he pulled out the tubes they'd stuck in him and pushed through the doctors and nurses until he found a glass. Raising it to his lips, the dehydrated man drank until he was satisfied.

Then the doctors began to staple his scalp back together.

• • •

Charles E. James, 36, had left a bloody trail in the west Orlando area.

He'd drifted from Fairgrove, Michigan, to Detroit, and then hoboed south. For the past few weeks, he'd stayed in homeless shelters in the Miami area, before moving up to Orlando.

He'd been there for approximately a month, living in shelters and eating at local soup kitchens. He panhandled for cash and committed burglaries and robberies to support his crack habit.

Police had been investigating two similar beatings, both savage and debilitating to the elderly victims. The first had occurred on the morning of December 7, 1993. A black male had entered Morgan Appliances on nearby Church Street and asked the owner for a job. When Charles Morgan stated that he didn't have a job opening, James asked for a dollar. As Morgan reached into his pocket to give the stranger four quarters, James punched him in the face. He proceeded to beat Morgan severely and stole nearly five hundred dollars from him.

The second encounter was even more violent. On the morning of December 26, James entered Haygood Bros., Inc., on Church Street and asked for a job. Seventy-four-year-old Lee Haygood stated that there were no jobs available. James then demanded that he be given a camera. When the owner refused to give it up, James beat Haygood over the head with a brick rolled up in a newspaper. Haygood was struck at least three times and knocked unconscious. Before leaving, James stole one hundred fifty dollars in cash. He left the brick in a trash can, and police were able to match his fingerprints to the attack at Morgan Appliances.

Lee Haygood sustained permanent injuries from the beating and suffered a stroke soon after.

Fingerprints from the three crime scenes were found to belong to Charles E. James.

• • •

A month later, Rick and Debbie Amoedo named their new son Nicholas Ricardo Amoedo, "Little NRA," dedicated to the National Rifle Association, whose policies Rick attributes to allowing him to have his gun when it was needed.

Later, he reflected on the horrifying experience:

"When I shot him [Charles E. James], I didn't pay any attention to him. I just wanted to go home and be with my family.

"[When I was robbed a year ago], I thought it was like a movie scene. I was just talking with my customers and these guys just ran in and said they wanted the money, and . . . the robbers took all [the customers'] jewelry and wallets. There were three, one had a 9 mm in my face. I let them have whatever they wanted. One of the other guys, a customer, was getting all nervous. He said, 'They're gonna shoot me,' and I said, 'Shut up!' He ended up crashing through the door, getting away from them. From then on, I said that is not gonna happen here again. That guy's [the robber] either going to jail or going under, 'cause it's not right.

"This guy [Charles E. James] was close to killing somebody. He burst a blood vessel in the old guy [Lee Haygood]."

A year after the attack, Rick was able to find a bit of humor in it.

"I don't know where I found the strength from," he said, "but I usually hit my head up and down on the cars out there all the time. If he'd hit me in the stomach, I'd probably bend over. It was a situation I didn't want to be in. But I had to take care of it."

11

The Pawnshop Robbery

"How did three million Germans put ten million men, women, and children in the ovens? Because Germany passed gun laws years before that took away all civilian guns. Will we ever learn?"
—Fred Prasse

The summer of 1978 was turning out to be a brutal one in St. Louis. Outside the Delmar Loan and Pawn Shop, heat shimmered on the asphalt. In the distance, thunderheads turned the sky purple.

In the inner city, pawnshops had become the favorite targets of armed robbers. As the summer wore on, the robbers became more violent. In May, Friedman Loan Company had been held up. The pawnbroker had resisted. In the gunfight that followed, both the owner and the bandit were killed. Friedman Loan was only two blocks from Delmar Pawn.

The bloody robbery served as a wake-up call to many business owners. They began tightening security.

At noon on July 7, 1978, Fred Prasse leaned against the counter, his back to the front door. Frank Van Almsick, owner of

Delmar Pawn, listened half heartedly as Prasse, 58, explained a new technique he'd developed to signal a silent alarm in case of robbery. The owner's wife waited on a trio of customers at the jewelry case. Another employee was stocking the display window, which looked out on Delmar Boulevard.

Prasse had recently bought Guardian Sentry Alarm Company. The former World War II veteran and retired cop had long held an interest in security systems.

By the late 1970s, silent alarms for businesses had become the rage. Holdup buttons, as they were called, had been so successful in alerting police to robberies in progress that criminals were getting wise. Because of this, robberies were becoming more violent.

A typical robbery scenario included three or four gunmen bursting full-tilt into a business, screaming that a holdup was going down. If a clerk so much as twitched, he or she ran the risk of being shot. The robbers assumed that any movement was an attempt to activate the holdup button.

Someone needed to invent a more discreet method of alerting police. Prasse had an idea that he thought could revolutionize the security alarm industry. In his prototype, he had taken a set of points off an old Pontiac and screwed them into the bottom of a cash drawer. Then he hooked a telephone stretch-cord to the points—the stretch in the cord allowed the drawer to open and close. The cord was then camouflaged and hooked up to an out-of-the-way alarm box.

A five-dollar bill was stuck between the points and the cash drawer. If a robber came into the store, the clerk would remove the bill and hand it over along with the other cash in the register.

When the five-dollar bill was removed, the automobile points would connect, thus activating the system. There were no bells, no flashing lights, nothing to warn the robber. The clerk could act naturally, with no unnecessary movements to alarm the robber.

As Prasse explained his system to Van Almsick, the pawnshop owner shrugged him off.

"I don't need it," he said. "I've been here ten years and never been robbed."

Just as he said those words, Van Almsick's face turned pale.

Prasse turned around and saw a man pointing a pistol in his face. My God, he thought, I'm in the middle of a holdup.

Prasse later recalled, "In defensive firearm shooting, the first thing we used to teach was, Don't shoot the wrong person. Mark your target. I looked at the robber and saw that he wore a pair of yellow pants. I was thinking he was by himself, so I decided to stop the guy. In my mind, I nicknamed him Yellow Pants."

The robber held what local cops called a "lemon-squeezer." The .32 caliber revolver was a small, cheap weapon popular among street gang members in the area. Prasse wondered what kind of dumb lug would try to hold somebody up with a peashooter.

He still hadn't seen the big guns.

As a retired cop, Prasse had a lifetime license to carry a firearm. Holstered at his side and covered by his sports jacket was a five-shot .38 snub-nosed Chief. This lightweight aluminum-framed pistol was easily concealed, yet big enough to take down a man.

The robber who held the .32 in Prasse's face wasn't masked. Prasse knew instantly that this spelled trouble. This either meant that he was stupider than most criminals, which certainly seemed possible, or he didn't plan to leave any witnesses.

Prasse didn't notice a second robber who stood behind Yellow Pants until the man yanked a gun out of a large paper sack. The former cop knew instantly it was a sixteen-gauge, double-barreled sawed-off shotgun. Now *that* was a dangerous weapon.

The robber stuck it to Prasse's temple. That gunman wasn't wearing a mask either.

He announced, "I'm gonna kill this guy if you don't hand over the money!"

He cocked both hammers of the shotgun. Everything in the store had slowed to a crawl. Van Almsick, still in shock, hadn't made a move to open the cash register. His wife had dropped to the floor behind the counter. Three customers also hugged the floor. Near the front door, the employee who had been working on the display window had ducked behind the display counter. Prasse saw that a third robber held a pistol to the employee's head.

The robber with the lemon-squeezer was losing patience with Van Almsick.

"Blow away these assholes!" he screamed.

Yellow Pants cocked the little gun, the metallic click echoing throughout the pawnshop.

That was all Prasse needed. He twisted his head out of the line of fire and raised his hands, knocking the shotgun away.

The gun went off, but Prasse never heard it. The concussion deafened him. He saw the orange streak, saw the glass counter explode, and watched Van Almsick dive behind what was left of it.

As he turned back, Prasse pulled his revolver from its holster and squeezed off a quick shot. Then he dived to the floor. The bullet hit the shotgun-wielding robber in the elbow, but the man pulled the second trigger and blasted another counter into tiny glass shards.

Prasse sat up and noticed he was holding his pistol with bloody hands. He thought it was blood from the gunman, though he couldn't see whether he'd even hit the guy. He didn't realize it at the time, but nineteen pellets had ripped through his hands.

Prasse fired again. He was puzzled. He considered himself a marksman, and the gunman was right in front of him, but he didn't see where he'd hit him. Oh, Jesus! he thought. Maybe I've mistakenly put blanks in my gun.

The robber grasped his empty shotgun by the barrel. With both hands, he swung the butt at Prasse. What's this guy doing? thought Prasse. He's like Don Quixote fighting windmills. Had the robber's intentions not been deadly, Prasse would have laughed.

"Kill them!" the shotgun-swinging robber screamed to his partners.

Prasse aimed for the man's chest and squeezed off his third round. This time, the bullet found its mark, and the cartridge wasn't a blank. The man swung around, wobbling. He dropped the shotgun and staggered toward the counter. Prasse saw him lurching toward Mrs. Van Almsick, who was still on the floor. He thought the robber planned to take her hostage. So he aimed at the middle of his back and fired again. This cartridge was a hollow point—the assailant dropped like a stone. The bullet entered his back and tore a baseball-size hole in his chest when it came out.

By now the third robber had opened fire. He had a .22 caliber Saturday Night Special. It popped like a cap gun when he fired it.

Every counter in the store had been shattered. The owner, his wife, and the clerk were hiding behind any cover they could find. The customers scrambled from one side of the shop to the other in an attempt to avoid the gunfire. Smoke and cordite rose to the ceiling.

But it wasn't over yet.

A section of the counter behind the cash register was still standing. Prasse leaped behind it. He spotted Yellow Pants near the front door. He had his lemon-squeezer aimed at Prasse. Pop, pop, pop went the little gun, like the flashbulb of an instamatic camera. The bullets whizzed by Prasse.

Prasse knew he had only one bullet left. He waited for Yellow Pants to stop shooting. Then he stood up, aimed for the head, and squeezed the trigger. The assailant sank to his knees in the doorway.

The third robber raced out the door and fled down the street.

Prasse needed to reload. He usually carried six extra rounds. He felt in his pocket for his other bullets. A sick feeling hit him. He'd forgotten them.

Yellow Pants was still kneeling in the doorway waving the lemon-squeezer in his hands. Prasse looked at him in amazement. The top of his head had been blown off. Blood gushed out of the wound, running like a stream across the floor. Still, he rubbed his forehead. My God! Prasse thought. Half his brains are blown out, and he's acting like he has a headache.

Prasse heard a car squeal to a stop at the front of the store. Two men jumped out and rushed through the front door.

Prasse could hear Frank Van Almsick throwing open what remaining drawers were left. Belatedly, he was looking for weapons.

"Throw me another gun!" Prasse yelled. "They're coming back!"

The two men grabbed Yellow Pants. They dragged him to the car, shoved him into the back seat, then sped away.

The clerk had finally found a gun. He heaved it across the counter. Prasse caught it. He noticed that it was an 1892 antique nine-inch Colt. After quickly checking it, he saw that it was loaded. He cocked it. The old gun was so heavy he had to balance it on what remained of the cash register. Prasse aimed it at the door and waited for the robbers to return for their other accomplice.

Across the street, two police officers had heard the shots. The first one to arrive was in uniform. Behind him, a plainclothes detective came in the door with his gun drawn. He was dressed similarly to one of the holdup men, and Prasse trained the old Colt on him.

Something, however, made him hesitate.

The officer quickly grasped what was happening. He pulled out his badge and yelled, "I'm a police officer. Don't shoot!"

Prasse breathed a sigh of relief before he lowered his weapon.

● ● ●

James Foston, 21, of North 18th Street, St. Louis, lay dead on the pawnshop floor. He was the leader of a local street gang and a suspected accomplice in several murders of rival gang members.

His criminal record included numerous arrests for burglary, robbery, and assault, as well as drug charges.

Patrick Harris (Yellow Pants), 21, of Dickson Street, was dropped off by his accomplices at Cochran Veteran's Hospital, just down the road from Delmar Loan and Pawn. Initially, he was listed in critical condition with a gunshot wound to the head. He later died.

Clyde Strong, 22, of Cass Avenue, was arrested soon after the gunfight. He was charged with assault with intent to kill with malice and attempted robbery with a deadly weapon. In subsequent interviews with the police, he stated that the robbers had hoped that only employees would be in the store when they went in. The gang members planned to kill them before they could hit holdup buttons, then walk away with enough money, jewelry, and guns to make them the most powerful gang in St. Louis.

When homicide detectives asked if they had a contingency plan in case there were customers in the store, Strong thought a minute and said, "We was gonna kill everybody." He was later convicted and sentenced to ten years in prison.

The driver of the getaway car was questioned but released due to a lack of evidence.

• • •

Twenty years later, Prasse still carries four no. 6 birdshot shotgun pellets in his right hand. Fifteen more pellets went through his two hands. The doctor who treated him said, "I'm amazed. I couldn't push a knitting needle through your hand nineteen times without hitting a nerve or bone."

The Monday after the shooting, Prasse appeared at a coroner's inquest. The proceedings lasted just seven minutes. After seeing Prasse's bandaged hands and hearing the facts of the case, the jury ruled that the shootings were justifiable homicide. They also remembered that numerous clerks in St. Louis had been gunned down recently by armed robbers.

Prasse stated, "The police can only get to a crime scene after the crime has been committed. A citizen must be able to stop a crime.

"The men who held up this store all had previous records and would have killed the owner, his wife, the clerk, and the customers. One guy admitted that to investigating officers. If I hadn't acted as I did, we wouldn't be here today."

12

The Stalker

"This guy doesn't take rejection lightly. . . ."
—Psychiatrist who analyzed Robert Stella

T he stalking had gone on for more than a year.

At some point during the ordeal, Judy Davis made up her mind to buy a pistol. She doesn't remember exactly when she made the decision. It may have been when she realized that the Orange County, Florida, Sheriff's Department could not protect her.

An acquaintance suggested that a large caliber bullet would stop a big man, and revolvers don't jam like automatics. For that reason, she chose a .38 Police Special.

Robert Stella stood over six feet tall and weighed two hundred pounds. He had straight black hair and brooding eyes. Davis had once thought him attractive. After a few dates, however, she'd come to realize that he was extremely possessive. He wanted to spend every waking hour with her. Stella even attempted to freeze out all of Davis's friends.

Davis soon grew tired of the constant, everyday assault on her freedom and ended the relationship. Stella let her know that he was unhappy with the decision. He stated that he would have her back one way or another.

The rejected suitor began his campaign with a barrage of late-night telephone calls. As soon as Davis would go to bed, the phone would ring. It was almost as if he were watching her. Sometimes when she answered the phone, Stella would try to coax her into taking him back. Other times, the caller would say nothing.

At first, Davis shrugged off the calls. Being an attractive, 49-year-old single woman, she was accustomed to men pursuing her. But she'd never dated anyone like Robert Stella. Davis knew it would be hard to trace his calls, if it came to that, because of Stella's expertise with telephone systems; he operated a business out of his home, brokering telephone services.

After a few weeks of harassing Davis at her home, Stella began calling her at work. Davis was a respected salesperson at Watson Realty in Orlando, Florida. Given the recent boom in the city's real estate market, she had been working hard just to keep pace. Her office was on Michigan Street, in the downtown area, but she traveled all over the city, showing homes and talking up sales. After Davis refused to take Stella's calls, he began stalking her.

On October 15, 1994, he stood in the shadows watching her house. At 8:15 P.M., Davis took her dog outside for a walk. Stella ran up and begged her to take him back. When she told him to leave her alone, he punched her. As she tried to pull away, he grabbed her hair. Davis screamed, trying to break free. But Stella held on. In a weird tug of war, Davis felt her hair being ripped from her scalp. She finally broke free and ran inside to call 911. Looking in the mirror, she saw patches of raw, bloody scalp where her hair should have been. She was horrified—Stella had actually pulled her hair out by the roots.

Police arrested Stella, charging him with trespass and criminal mischief. After the police left, Davis found her keys missing. Stella spent only a few hours in jail.

The telephone calls became more insistent, turning to threats and taunts. By now Davis had become a psychological hostage to a terrorist. She didn't feel safe, even inside her apartment. She couldn't concentrate on her job and thought of nothing but Stella and his threats.

On November 11, 1994, Davis was home alone when she heard someone knocking on the back door. She walked to the bathroom, where the door was located, and saw Stella standing outside, trying to beat down the door. The pounding became so loud that the walls of her apartment shook.

"Let me in!" he screamed.

Davis grabbed a portable phone and fled through the front door. She called 911, but by the time police arrived, Stella had fled. Orange County sheriff's deputies searched the neighborhood but could find no sign of the stalker.

As soon as they left, Davis heard footsteps on her porch. She peered through the peephole and saw Stella crouching outside her front door. She called 911 again, and this time deputies found him nearby. He was arrested and charged with burglary and stalking.

After this brush with the law, Stella decided that direct contact with Davis was dangerous. He spent the next several months bombarding her answering machine with threats and obscenities. Although he threatened to kill her, he did not venture close enough to get arrested again. Davis used her answering machine to screen calls. She never answered the telephone at home anymore until she knew the caller was not Stella.

On March 30, 1995, Davis was working in her office at Watson Realty when she looked out the window and saw Stella hiding in some bushes. Terrified, she called 911. Coworkers gathered protectively around her as she waited for the police.

True to the pattern he'd established, Stella ran down the street, got in his car, and drove away. Police searched the area but failed to locate him.

The embarrassment to Davis was overwhelming. In this latest incident, her coworkers and customers had become involved. Now she began to wonder if she would lose her job because of the stalker.

Although her mind wasn't on her work, Davis completed her duties and began driving home. She usually found the drive relaxing. Because of her flexible schedule, she rarely had to drive during the rush hours. But seeing Stella again had made her apprehensive. She just wanted to get home so she could try to unwind.

A few blocks away from her office, she noticed a late-model white Cadillac following her. She knew instantly that it was Robert Stella. She cursed herself for not having a cellular telephone in her car. Through her rearview mirror she watched as he remained a few car-lengths behind. Nearby, she remembered, was a secluded suburb where she'd shown property. In an attempt to elude her pursuer, she swung into the suburb.

As she cruised the quiet streets, Stella suddenly sped past her vehicle. His car was a blur as it swung directly in front of her. His tires smoked as he screeched to a stop.

Davis jammed on her brakes and stopped a few feet short of

ramming the Cadillac. Stella lunged from his car and raced toward her. His face, silhouetted in the street lights, was contorted with rage. Davis quickly locked the doors, but Stella repeatedly punched the side window. His fist seemed oblivious to the hard glass.

"Help me! Somebody please help!" Davis screamed.

Stella finally succeeded in breaking the window. Impervious to a bloody fist, he reached through the glass and began slamming her face with jackhammer blows.

Davis slumped to the other side of the seat, trying to avoid his fists. The assailant then climbed up on the hood and began kicking the windshield. He stood directly above the steering wheel as his kicks rocked Davis's car.

She knew she had to get help. She looked around the neighborhood, but no one was coming. Lights were beginning to flash on in the surrounding houses, and she prayed that someone would at least call the police.

Davis leaned on her horn, sounding an eerie wail into the neighborhood. The windshield suddenly crashed in around her, and she groped for the door handle on the passenger side. But Stella was too fast. He grabbed her arm and wrenched her from the car. Then he pulled her to him and began kissing her.

"Help! Help me!"

Davis saw a movement to her left. A man and woman were rushing toward them.

"Hey buddy, let her go," the man said.

"Wanna be a hero?" Stella shouted at the intruder.

The man dived into the fight. He and Stella and Davis struggled on the street for what was only a few seconds but seemed like an hour. At last, the samaritan managed to pull Stella's hands away from Davis. As soon as she was free, she raced for the nearest house. Bruised and shaking, she called 911.

By the time deputies from the Orange County Sheriff's Department arrived, Stella had fled.

Deputies reasoned that an insane man might return to his victim's apartment, and several were dispatched to stake it out. Sure enough, Stella was spotted hiding in the bushes outside her bedroom window. A chase ensued, but the suspect vanished into the night. Two K-9s were brought in to assist in the search, and within minutes the spotlight from a police helicopter scanned the area for the stalker.

A deputy had spotted Stella's car parked two blocks away from the victim's house. The deputy waited in the shadows until he saw Stella steal out of the trees and approach his car. Cops quickly swooped down on the suspect.

Davis was driven by a deputy from the crime scene to her house. When asked to identify the suspect, she quickly pointed to Stella.

As he saw the identification being made, the stalker told an officer, "I can't handle this. I'm out of control."

Davis couldn't have agreed more.

Stella was served with papers to prevent him from having contact with her. He was advised to stay at least a mile away.

Less than a week later, he was back, this time driving a white 1995 Chevrolet Blazer. He began his pursuit when Davis turned west on Curry Ford Road.

As they raced through the early morning traffic, it all hit Davis at once. The never-ending telephone calls, the relentless stalking, the beatings, the desperate fear that never really left her. She began to hyperventilate. Weak from exhaustion, she began to sob.

Davis was within a few blocks of Florida Hospital, so she drove into the emergency room parking lot. A nurse helped her call police. After treatment for stress, doctors released her, and she went home.

Stella was again charged with aggravated stalking and criminal mischief. In a police report dated April 5, 1995, Orange County Deputy Paul Pacquette wrote, "The victim is in fear for her life, and it is the opinion of this writer the victim has cause to be in fear. Defendant was arrested 03-31-95 for aggravated stalking and arrested this date for same charge. Defendant is obsessed and stated so. During my two-hour investigation, victim's fear was genuine. This deputy fears for her well-being."

Pacquette was so impressed by the seriousness of the situation that he called the Orange County judge under whose jurisdiction the case would be tried and advised him that Robert Stella was dangerous and was likely to commit acts of violence against Davis. The judge set bond at $125,000 and stated that the "defendant was not to be released at lower bond without a bond reduction hearing."

Stella pleaded no contest and was released after being sentenced to three years probation with counseling.

Judy Davis had long suspected that the criminal court system would not protect her. After months of calling the police and obtaining court orders to keep her stalker away, he had not been locked up for more than a few days. This latest court action convinced her that she could not rely on the court. She would have to protect herself.

•••

The prolonged stalking and harassment had taken a toll on Davis. She was always exhausted. She was sure her coworkers and customers could sense the strain she felt, and she continually worried about keeping her job.

On September 21, 1995, Stella was again arrested for trespassing. This time, he'd stood outside Davis's window glaring at her.

The court system was obviously as insane as Stella. Three days later, when Davis came home from work, he was there again. As she turned on the bedroom light, she sensed movement and saw her stalker smiling at her.

"Get out of here!" she screamed.

Stella didn't move.

"You don't live here. Leave!"

When Stella lunged for her, Davis ran from the apartment and called 911 on a portable telephone.

Investigating officers found Stella hiding in the bathroom. He tried to flee, but officers quickly overtook him. In his pocket, they found a screwdriver and an awl.

Stella was charged with burglary of an occupied dwelling, possession of burglary tools, and repeated violation of an injunction to stay away from Davis. Officers discovered that he had jimmied the bathroom door and entered while Davis was away.

This time, Stella spent forty-five days in the Orange County Jail.

On November 8, he appeared before Orange County Circuit Judge Dorothy Russell. Judy Davis watched the proceedings with disbelief. Here was a man who had threatened to kill her numerous times, had committed many acts of physical violence against her, had broken into her home on several occasions, and had carried an awl and screwdriver the last time. Those tools were more frightening to Davis than a knife. She could imagine what an unbalanced man could do with such weapons.

Judge Russell asked Stella if he would "behave" if freed. Stella nodded. His attorney quickly stated that he would plead "no contest" to violation of probation, burglary, and violating court orders in return for leniency.

Russell sentenced Stella to fifteen years' probation and ordered him to stay at least one mile away from Davis. And he was ordered to attend a counseling program that dealt specifically with rejection.

Davis had seen and read of many cases in which stalkers were not taken seriously by the courts, and several had ended up killing their victims. She had never fired a gun, but now she thought of the pistol as a friend. She would sit up at night staring at it—the shiny steel barrel, the bullets thick as a man's finger, the explosion that shocks the ears when it is fired.

She'd finally made up her mind. If the Orange County courts refused to protect her, she would protect herself.

The stalking had gone on for more than a year. But now Davis was determined to put an end to it. The layers of fear and guilt and embarrassment had coalesced into a wall of strength.

She felt a debt of gratitude to the Orange County Sheriff's Department. They had always responded quickly to her calls and had treated her with kindness. Many officers had gone out of their way to patrol her neighborhood and place of business. Others had warned judges about the deadly threat posed by Stella. The

Orange County Sheriff's Department could not, however, keep Stella in jail.

On November 14, 1995, six days after Robert Stella had told Orange County Circuit Judge Dorothy Russell that he would "behave," Davis was outside walking her dog when she saw Stella charging at her. The time was exactly 10:21 P.M.

For a moment, Davis stood in shock. Then fear overtook her, and she turned and raced toward her house. She dragged her dog by the collar. Its squeals pierced the quiet night.

Stella followed.

She yanked open the front door to her apartment, darted inside, and slammed it shut. Outside, she heard Stella pounding on it. She'd flicked at the deadbolt lock as she entered, but in her fear, hadn't set it properly.

She knew Stella would quickly disable the lock and enter her house. Davis released the dog and ran straight toward her bedroom.

As she pulled the .38 from beneath her pillow, Davis heard the door bang open. She raced back out into the living room and saw Stella entering through the front door.

"Stop or I'll shoot!"

As she pointed the gun at him, Stella hesitated.

"Leave my house!"

Stella didn't seem to recognize the change in Davis. She stood tall and confident, her eyes steely, her face flushed with anger.

Her hands held the gun without shaking.

The stalker and the victim stood a few feet apart. Stella's eyes were glassy, as if he'd been using drugs. A sneer slowly formed on his lips.

"*Leave or I'll shoot,*" Davis shouted.

Stella didn't hesitate any longer.

He rushed Davis.

She almost waited too long. She felt him brush against her, and she twisted away. She aimed the gun at his chest and fired.

Once it went off, the gun seemed to have a mind of its own. It didn't want to stop firing. A half-dozen explosions rocked the apartment. Smoke and cordite steamed to the ceiling.

Stella crumpled to the floor, his eyes staring at Davis in disbelief.

"Ohmygodohmygodohmygod," he mumbled.

Now Davis fell apart. The gun shook in her hands, and a whimper escaped from her. She dropped the pistol on the sofa and began sobbing.

Through blurred vision, she watched Stella crawl through the doorway. Like a dog hit by a car, he dragged away, leaving bloody swaths across the floor.

Davis picked up the telephone and dialed 911 without even looking at the numbers.

Within minutes, Orange County deputies arrived. They sealed off the house and called detectives. Then they began a search for Davis's attacker. As usual, Stella was gone. But this time there was a trail of blood to follow.

Davis went into shock. She slumped onto the sofa, sobbing hysterically. A policewoman comforted her as they waited for detectives to arrive. She stated over and over, "I've killed him."

The search dragged on for two hours. Police had quickly located Stella's car a few blocks away. Several officers staked it out and waited for the wounded man to return.

K-9s, by now familiar with Stella's scent, were called in. Within a few minutes, he was found lying on a doorstep a block away.

He looked up at the officer and said, "I can't believe she shot me." The deputy could only shake his head.

When the ambulance arrived, paramedics lifted Stella onto a stretcher and rushed him to Orlando Regional Medical Center.

• • •

Judy Davis was not charged with any crime. She feels that the Orange County criminal justice system left her no alternative but to shoot Stella. She'd filled out statements. She'd obtained court orders to keep him away. She'd testified against him in court. Finally, she was forced to take matters into her own hands.

Robert Stella was held under armed guard at the Orlando Regional Medical Center until he recuperated from wounds to his chest and right forearm.

On November 16, while still in the hospital, he was served with a warrant charging him with aggravated stalking and burglary.

The court had finally had enough. After leaving the hospital, Stella was sentenced to fifteen years in prison, with no chance of parole until he has served 85 percent of his sentence.

Judy Davis remains skeptical. She still keeps her .38 under her pillow, cocked and loaded.

13

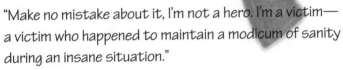

The Abduction

"Make no mistake about it, I'm not a hero. I'm a victim—
a victim who happened to maintain a modicum of sanity
during an insane situation."
—Paul Brite

It was 7:00 A.M. on July 24, 1995. Paul Brite wheeled his late-model Lexus into the Amoco service station in Coral Springs, Florida. Brite, a 53-year-old businessman, used his credit card to top off the tank, then drove to the east side of the station for the free car wash that came with a fill-up.

No one else was in line. The car wash was separated from the pumps by an eight-foot-high concrete wall. Brite rolled his window down to enter the four-digit code that was printed on his gas receipt. As he punched in the numbers, he saw a teenage boy idling nearby. The young man wore blue jeans and a tight T-shirt. A baseball cap was tilted on his head. Brite assumed he was an employee of the gas station.

Water and foam from a previous customer slicked the concrete driveway beneath the heavy automatic car wash brushes. Brite was in a hurry. He was CEO of the Fast Bolt Florida Corporation located in the industrial section of Coral Springs. He was on his way to an early meeting.

Coral Springs is a modern city on Florida's "Gold Coast." It is located in Broward County, near Fort Lauderdale. Thirty years ago, the village was planned as a model community, but recent urban sprawl is rapidly undermining its social foundation.

When Brite tapped in the last digit, the green light lit up. He drove into the car wash and watched as the water began to spray his car. While waiting, he used the cell phone on the console to call his wife. About three minutes into their conversation, he noticed the same young man approaching his car. Brite told his wife, "I'll call you back when I finish washing the car."

Paul Brite, a Coral Springs, Florida, business owner who was kidnapped at gunpoint while driving through a car wash at a local service station.

He cracked the window, and the young man said, "You'll have to pull forward. The machine isn't working right. It won't reach the back of the vehicle."

Brite thanked him and pulled up. The brushes began to spin, thumping the back of the Lexus and showering rainbows of water against it.

The young man walked up close to the car again. When the driver didn't acknowledge him, he tapped on the window. Brite wondered if there could be another problem. He rolled down the window, only to find himself looking into the barrel of a revolver. It was camouflaged in a plastic grocery bag, but the barrel looked huge. Brite, a gun afficionado, had no doubt that it was a pistol.

"The biggest revolver on earth," he later recalled, "is the one pointed at your head."

"Turn off the car!" his assailant snapped.

After Brite switched off the ignition, the man motioned with the gun and said, "Get in the passenger seat!"

"I can't. The console's too high."

The assailant jerked open the door and grabbed Brite's arm. Holding his weapon in the startled man's face, he yanked him out of the car.

A string of obscenities were hurled at Brite before the gunman got down to business.

"Gimme your money!"

Brite pulled a wad of bills from his pocket and handed it over.

"Now your wallet," the gunman said.

The assailant took Brite's keys and watch. Then he took his wedding band.

The ring on Brite's pinky finger had been given to him by a favorite uncle. "May I keep this one?" he requested lamely. "It's a family heirloom."

The assailant jammed the weapon hard against Brite's temple.

"Hand it over!" he demanded, and Brite quickly complied.

Next, the gunman yanked at three thick gold chains the victim was wearing around his neck. When he couldn't jerk them loose, he flashed a menacing smile.

"I'll take those later," he said. The meaning was not lost on Brite.

Brite later recounted the experience. "He's not speaking softly. He's shouting in my face. He's ordering me where to go, what to do. Or, he says, 'I will kill you!' He's peppering everything with obscenities, gutter language of the basest sort."

He forced Brite around to the back of the car and opened the trunk. "You got anything in there?" the assailant asked.

"No, nothing," Brite lied.

"I knew I had two pistols in the trunk," Brite remembered. "A friend and I had made arrangements to go to a Palm Beach shooting range later in the week. It was a new police electronic target range. We were looking forward to checking it out."

Brite had used firearms since he was a child. His father trained police officers in proper shooting techniques, and Brite himself had been cited for proficiency at various levels with both handguns and rifles. But he never hunted—he hated to kill animals.

A fully loaded Ruger .357 Magnum and a Mauser HCS .32 with a six-shot magazine were in a briefcase in the trunk.

The gunman placed the pistol against Brite's chest and screamed, "Get in the trunk!"

Brite breathed a sigh of relief, and hopped in instantly. Had he not known the guns were in there, he would have refused to budge. He was all too aware that people usually end up dead when they are kidnapped from a populated area at gunpoint. Even with cold fear clawing at him, Brite had the presence of mind to fall on top of the satchel that held the guns. It looked more like a brief-case than a guncase, and the assailant didn't notice it.

"I was fighting hysteria," he later said. "I was fighting fear. I knew for a certainty that this young man was going to kill me."

The assailant slammed the trunk shut.

The small space was pitch-black, a darkness imagined only in nightmares. The cramped quarters made his shoulder ache. In order to orient himself, he allowed his fingers to move about the trunk. The carpet had the consistency of wool. The metal of the trunk lid felt like ice. The only thing that consoled him was the gun case beneath his body.

He was surprised that he could hear everything that went on outside the car. Another car pulled up, and his abductor said, "He's in the trunk."

The reply was inaudible, then the gunman answered, "Follow me."

The engine started, and the Lexus pulled away.

"We're going to your house," the assailant said to Brite. Even though the voice was muffled, the businessman was amazed that they could carry on a dialog.

"We can't go to my house," Brite told him.

"Who's at your house?"

"My three sons and my dogs."

184 THE BEST DEFENSE

"I need money!" the kidnapper shrieked. "Get me some money!"

Brite could hear the engines of automobiles passing his car. *Where are we going?* he wondered. *What if he turns and shoots through the back seat? If he does, I'm dead.*

What would happen if he died? His wife would have to run the business or sell it. His sons would have to grow up without him. His oldest would be entering college soon, and could make a life, but what about his two younger sons?

And what if the gunman dumped his body where no one ever found it? Would his family think he'd just gotten tired of the rat race and deserted them? And what about his wife? Would she think he'd run off with another woman? But those kinds of possibilities were endless. He decided to stop thinking about them.

Brite opened the gun case and felt a surge of confidence when his fingers touched the handguns. He placed the .357 Magnum in his right hand and the Mauser in his left. Years before, he'd had surgery on his neck and because of nerve damage had lost much of the use of his left hand. He didn't know if he could even squeeze the trigger of the Mauser, but the .357 Magnum would make the question academic.

The gunman suddenly shouted back to him, "Where's your car phone?"

Brite didn't answer right away. His cell phone was on the console beside the driver's seat. Surely the kidnapper had seen it. The question confused Brite until he realized the gunman thought he had a cell phone in the trunk.

"I don't have a cell phone," Brite answered.

"I know you have one!"

"No, I don't."

Brite felt every turn of the Lexus, heard every car on the highway that passed them or came toward them. If he could find some way to signal, he might have a chance. So near and yet so far, he thought. The old cliché seemed more appropriate now than he'd ever imagined it could.

The businessman groped about in the darkness for the brake lights. If he could turn them on somehow, a motorist might pick up his SOS. But he soon realized the Lexus was built too well—there were no loose wires to connect. And there was no inside lock in the trunk that he might open.

He was trapped. Brite was stuck in a waiting game, and he could hear the clock ticking down. What if the kidnapper drove the car into a canal and simply walked away? He remembered a case a few years back when four teenagers disappeared. Their parents thought they'd been kidnapped, had searched for them all those years. Then eight years later, when a canal near Miami was being dredged, the car was found with the four bodies inside. They'd been there all along—victims of an unfortunate traffic accident.

"I *know* you got a cell phone," the kidnapper shouted again.

"No, I don't."

Brite tried to remain docile. If the kidnapper felt threatened, the businessman was dead. The assailant could easily turn and shoot through the back seat. If he decided to do that, there was nowhere to hide.

In his mind, Brite pictured the car being driven to the Everglades, a swamp filled with all kinds of hostile creatures. Man-eating alligators. Poisonous cottonmouth water moccasins. Encephalitic bloodsucking mosquitoes.

He wanted to pound the trunk with his fists, and scream at the top of his lungs for somebody to come help him. But he knew that would be suicidal.

To calm himself, he checked his weapons again. The .357 was loaded with Black Talons, a devastating round that could take down an elephant. This was the gun he would use if he were given a chance. The Mauser would be used only for backup. Brite derived some comfort in just holding on to the guns.

"You got a car phone back there, don't you?" the kidnapper asked for the third time. Brite decided that the gunman had cell phones on the brain.

The car slowed, then stopped. Everything became silent. Brite heard the door slam, and then footsteps were coming toward him. He placed both guns at the ready and waited.

The trunk popped open and Brite lunged out. The kidnapper was stunned by the victim who suddenly faced him. Brite held two pistols, both aimed at the gunman's chest.

"People ask me why I didn't shoot him as soon as the trunk opened," Brite said. "The answer is I didn't know it was him. It could have been a police officer. We could have been in a school-yard." And he was momentarily blinded by the sunlight.

"Put your hands on your head and get down on the ground!" Brite ordered. He could see shapes now, but still couldn't distinguish features.

The assailant ignored the warning and, with his right hand, reached for his pocket.

Brite fired a warning shot into the air.

BOOM!

"Do what I say! Get down on the ground!"

The man again reached for his pocket, but more slowly this time.

BOOM!

The assailant didn't seem to realize the danger that the .357 Magnum represented.

The gunman reached for his pocket again.

BOOM!

Brite had fired three warning shots above the head of his attacker. But the man just stood there, unresponsive. Brite could see clearly now, and he kept his eyes on his attacker's hands.

Then the right hand darted downward, like a western gunfighter slapping leather. Instinctively, Brite lowered the .357 Magnum. When the barrel reached the level of the man's thigh, he pulled the trigger.

BOOM!

Brite intended to knock the man down and disable him. He did not shoot to kill.

The attacker staggered.

As Brite later said, "There were no movie-type dramatics. No spinning around. No screaming. No being blown backward six feet. He just staggered."

The attacker went down to a knee. "Now get down on the ground," Brite told him.

"I'm shot!"

Brite thought he'd missed.

"You're not shot," he said.

"Let me show you," the gunman insisted.

"Pull your pants down," Brite said. He'd seen a cop say that in a movie once. The theory was that if a man's trousers were bunched around his ankles, he couldn't run. Kind of like hobbling a horse, Brite thought.

"Don't kill me," the attacker whined. "I'm only a kid."

"You're not hit."

Brite noted the transformation. A minute earlier his captive had been a swaggering aggressor, profane and menacing.

The assailant lifted up his shirt, and Brite saw the bullet hole. The abductor had been struck in the right side, higher up than Brite had aimed. There was little bleeding, and the attacker did not moan. Only the shock in the man's eyes and the bullet hole told Brite that his shot had found its mark.

"Keep your hands up," Brite warned, "or I'll blow your head off."

Brite glanced at his surroundings. To the east was a canal, behind which sat an industrial district. But on the other side, beyond a row of trees, was a trailer park. That seemed to be his closest avenue of assistance.

"Somebody call the police!" Brite yelled as loud as he could.

He saw no movement to indicate that anyone heard him, so he hollered louder. Usually soft-spoken, Brite yelled as loud as he could.

"*Somebody call the police!*"

A car drove up. Two teenagers in the front seat stared at the man with the gun.

"Call the police," Brite commanded. "I've been kidnapped and need assistance."

The driver seemed uninterested. Or maybe he was just confused or frightened. He gunned the engine and sped away.

Two youngsters on bicycles pedaled toward the scene. "Get out of here!" Brite shouted, then felt a strange need to explain his gruffness. Pointing to the assailant lying in the street, he said, "He's got a gun and might shoot you."

The kids scattered.

From the corner of his eye, Brite saw an old clunker slowly sputtering toward him. It was a dusty, banged-up Chevelle station wagon that looked like it had traveled down some hard roads. He remembered it from the car wash where he'd been kidnapped.

The car drew closer, and Brite watched it warily, all the time trying to keep the wounded gunman in sight. The car coughed and belched and began to speed up. Now it was coming straight at him.

But Brite was ready. He leaped sideways just before it would have plowed into him.

The car smoked to a stop, and the driver began to roll down the passenger window. Brite sensed that he was going to be shot. He raised the .32 caliber revolver and fired at the door. The bullet slammed into the molding just below the window. Glass flew everywhere.

That was enough for the driver. The old station wagon jerked away in a cloud of black smoke. His attacker was lying on the ground now, moaning. Brite glanced at him, then watched the station wagon smoking off into the distance.

At last he heard sirens.

Looking down the street, he saw a procession of police cars headed his way. Their blue lights flashed against the palm trees that lined the canal. Checking his downed assailant once again, Paul Brite breathed a sigh of relief.

● ● ●

The first squad car screeched to a stop. An officer jumped out and drew his weapon. Using his door as a shield, he leveled his revolver at Brite. The businessman dropped both guns as ordered and placed his hands on his head.

"By now police cars were dropping out of the sky. A dozen officers had their guns trained on me. They were all screaming directions. They told me move backward four steps, then get down on my knees," said Brite.

Despite the pain from the nerve damage in his neck, Brite did as he was told. He realized that the police didn't know him and couldn't be sure that he wouldn't turn on them and begin firing.

Brite was quickly handcuffed and led to a police car. The cuffs dug into his wrists, and he asked the officer to loosen them. He also asked for a cigarette, which was placed between his lips. While he told his story, an ambulance arrived and paramedics loaded the suspect onto a stretcher. Brite watched it roar away in a wave of flashing crimson lights.

At the Coral Springs Police Department, Brite was informed that his assailant had died at North Broward Medical Center in Fort Lauderdale. The bullet from Brite's .357 Magnum had ripped through the abdomen, just above the thigh, and tore into the femoral artery. Shortly after arriving at the hospital, he'd bled to death.

The assailant's name was Carl Lee Reese, 21. He'd been arrested numerous times and convicted of car-jacking, burglary, robbery and assault with a deadly weapon. He'd recently been released from a South Carolina prison. Further investigation into Reese's background revealed that he was a fugitive, wanted in South Carolina and Palm Beach County for violation of parole.

In the meantime, Coral Springs police had relayed a BOLO (Be On the Lookout) call for the accomplice's vehicle. Coral Springs police officer Karl Milenkovic was waiting at the traffic light on the corner of Coral Ridge and University Avenue when he observed a dirty Chevelle station wagon pull up beside him. Looking closer, the patrolman noticed a bullet hole in the passenger door and a shattered window. Milenkovic called for backup, then stopped the automobile. The driver, not surprisingly, turned out to be Reese's accomplice, 17-year-old Mario Denele Sikes.

As a minor, the surviving kidnapper was subject to a hearing in juvenile court, where he could receive as a maximum penalty incarceration in a juvenile facility until his eighteenth birthday. Then he must be released.

But a provision in Florida criminal statutes provides that, in exceptional circumstances, a juvenile defendant can be remanded to Circuit Court to be tried as an adult. The provision was deemed by the court to have been triggered in this instance.

Sikes was later tried and convicted of second degree murder (under Florida law, an accomplice can be charged with murder if anyone, including the perpetrator, is killed during the commission of a felony). He was given fifteen years.

• • •

Paul Brite recently spoke of the horror of his experience, which he relives every day of his life. "I had every justification for shooting him. He was going to kill me. I knew that, because his eyes told me. The police also told me that there was no alternative except to let him kill me. But it doesn't make it easier."

Brite is not a vindictive person. He has an active conscience and plenty of room for self-doubt. "It's been two and a half years," he said. "I did everything I could not to kill him. Believe me, the first shot would have gone straight into his chest if I had wanted it to. The man was eight feet from me. Now I don't claim to be Robin Hood, but I am a very proficient shot. If I shoot at something that close, I hit it.

"The judge at the trial asked me what kind of sentence I expected. I told him I'd already had too much responsibility thrust on me."

He thought for a moment, then said, "But fifteen years for second degree murder, kidnapping, car-jacking, and aggravated assault? That's outrageous.

"Quite frankly, had I not known that I had those guns back there, I would never have gotten in the trunk. Those weapons saved my life. I'm not as young as I once was, I'm not as strong as I was, I'm not as fast as I was. But if he'd gotten me, he would have found out that I would have gotten a piece of him, too!

"I value my responsibility to my wife, my family, and my company."

Brite ended the conversation by saying, "The police told me I did what I had to do. Otherwise, he would have killed me. All of that should make it real easy, but somehow it doesn't."

14

Last Ride of the Dixie Mafia

"Keeping weapons on the premises should be avoided. Statistics prove that having weapons on your property adds to the danger during a robbery."
—*Flyer provided to Beverly Hills Jewelers by Henrico County, Virginia, Police Department two weeks before the attempted armed robbery*

"The morning of December 2, 1994, started like any other day at my store," Gary B. Baker testified before the March 31, 1995, United States Congressional Hearings on Crime. "But it would end like no other day."

When Baker established Beverly Hills Jewelers in September 1987, he knew that dealing in gold and diamonds could make him a target. He designed the upscale facility with security as a leading concern.

"From the very beginning," the Richmond, Virginia, businessman later explained, "I did as much as I could to ensure that if there was a problem, my employees and I would survive by fighting back and not placing our lives at the mercy of vicious killers.

"We didn't want the jewelry store to look like a fort, but at the same time, we did as many little things as possible to discourage potential robbers."

Gary Baker knew that one day his subur-
ban jewelry store would likely be the target
of armed robbers. On Friday, December 2,
1994, when two masked gunmen raided
Beverly Hills Jewelers, he and his employees
were prepared.

Baker came up with a novel
blueprint: the glass display counters were raised five feet high and
linked to form a giant, squared-
off horseshoe. A four-foot walk-
way between the back of these
counters and the outside walls allowed store personnel to move
about freely. Customers were prevented from walking behind
these glass counters by four-and-a-half-foot-high solid wood
counters with locked doors.

Spaced every ten feet along the back sides of the showcases
were pistols—their butts turned out for quick and easy grasping.
All were .38 caliber revolvers, and all were fully loaded.

In the middle of the horseshoe, out on the sales floor, was a
similarly constructed fifteen-foot by fifteen-foot mini sales area.

As a backup precaution, Baker instructed his sales force not to
unnecessarily wander from their assigned stations, thus assuring
that each section of the store's perimeter and its middle were
always protected. An array of silent alarm buttons, wired into a
private security company, were spaced throughout the store.

Baker's office sits at the rear of the store, beyond the neck
of the horseshoe. It was elevated and faced the sales floor. While

sitting, a steel-plated panel concealed Baker's torso, but not his head. From this platform, he could survey every transaction as it happened.

Baker never doubted that his business might one day be targeted for robbery. "Certain things that I thought *would* happen, *did* happen. First, jewelers know that December is the killing season. Unfortunately, criminals also come to shop—their way—alongside our decent citizens. Second, I always guessed that if we got hit, it would be by professionals, and it would be in the early morning. They know that when stores are just opening up, people are psychologically off guard. Employees are wanting a cup of coffee, maybe a bite to eat. Part of these criminal predators' job is to know the ways of [their] human prey."

On that cold December morning, an attempted robbery that would help rewrite Virginia's gun laws was about to happen.

● ● ●

The cancer started in Biloxi, Mississippi, in the mid-1960s. Word went out across the states of the Old Confederacy, and the response was immediate: hoodlums, killers, safecrackers, and con men arrived by car and boat, foot and thumb. They came from places with names like Parchman and Raiford, Angola and Huntsville.

It was a full house, according to the grapevine. The sheriff, chief of police, mayor, and county judge had all been bought and paid for, and the city was open for business.

The newcomers didn't waste any time. They first infected the nerve center of Biloxi. The Strip, as it was called, hunkered low and ugly along U.S. Highway 90, a squalid stretch of striptease joints, porno booths, cheap motels, and bars. Traveling criminals made the Strip their home, taking over the gambling, bootlegging, prostitution, and drug dealing.

Airmen from nearby Kessler Air Base who wanted to party ended up with empty pockets and bruised bodies. Floating card games and crapshoots went on nonstop. And if a visitor wanted feminine companionship, he could always play a hand of venereal roulette for a twenty-dollar bill.

The Dixie Mafia, as the newcomers were soon called, began to spread to other cities and states. When the pickings were slim, they turned on each other to rob and kill.

One of the players in this high-stakes game was a career criminal named William "Pappy" Head, whose first recorded conviction was for a 1942 series of bank robberies in Mississippi. After serving several prison sentences throughout the 1940s, 1950s, and early 1960s, Head arrived in Biloxi and became a full-fledged member of the Dixie Mafia. His specialty at this time was robbing banks. He also would contract out to burn buildings so their owners could collect insurance premiums. Another pastime was murdering cohorts in the organization who got out of line. During one of his stretches in prison, a social worker labeled the aging murderer as "violence looking for a plot."

In early 1988, Biloxi judge Vince Sherry and his wife, Margaret, were gunned down inside their spacious home. Margaret Sherry was an anticorruption candidate for mayor at the time she was murdered. The FBI was ordered to investigate the murders. Special agents showed up to pound the pavements of the

Mississippi Gold Coast, and Dixie Mafia members scattered to all corners of the United States. Four members of the organization were later hunted down, tried for conspiracy to commit those murders, and convicted.

When the Feds arrived, Pappy Head and his best friend, Weldon "Casper the Ghost" Fossey, decided to try their luck in Texas. Fossey had earned his nickname in prison, where he'd been a hit man for Dixie Mafia interests within the system. When he murdered an inmate, he would wear a sack over his head so fellow convicts could truthfully say they hadn't seen who committed the murder. Then the guards would wink and ruefully intone, "It must have been a ghost."

Head and Fossey, along with a few associates, bought a secluded stretch of property in Hardin County, down near the Rio Grande. They wasted no time in building what authorities termed a "dope turnaround," which was nothing more than a circular driveway alongside a warehouse. An eighteen-wheeler could pull up, load or unload tons of marijuana, then be gone in a matter of minutes. The drugs were shipped to Florida, South Carolina, and Michigan for distribution nationwide.

Pappy Head and his cronies were prospering as they never had before. But there was a problem, and Head was chosen to eliminate it.

The problem was Weldon Fossey. A deranged Fossey was out of control. He would murder friends or strangers just to watch them die. In 1989, after he blew his top and shot one of his partners in the drug ring, Head and other members of the organization became afraid of him.

Fossey was executed with a shot to the back of the head, and an informant fingered Head as the triggerman. He fled Texas, only to be arrested later in Alabama. In his home, detectives discovered police uniforms, badges, and handcuffs. In addition to the police paraphernalia, authorities found a safecracker's kit, instructions for manufacturing methamphetamines, automatic weapons, police scanners, walkie-talkies, facial disguises, and bomb-making components.

Head was charged with murder but pleaded down to conspiracy to commit murder. In 1990, he was sentenced to five years in prison. However, the aging convict was released to his son's supervision just one year later. Had he served his full sentence, Head would have been in prison at the time he tried to rob Baker's jewelry store.

Thomas Jefferson Salter was never an official member of the Dixie Mafia, though he'd run in many of the same criminal circles as Head. Salter's son said his father thrived on the "thrill" and "fear" of committing crimes. For him, "it was a hell of an adrenaline rush." In a criminal life that spanned nearly forty years, he had been convicted of armed robbery, kidnapping, breaking and entering, and grand larceny. In 1983, Salter was sentenced to fifteen years for armed robbery. After serving only seven years in a North Carolina prison, Salter was released in 1990.

Two years later, he stole a $100,000 collection of rare stamps from a North Carolina philatelist and sold them to a woman in Dallas. They were later recovered, and he was charged with interstate transportation of stolen goods. But Salter didn't stay around to be tried. The interstate aspect of this crime made him a fugitive of the FBI.

According to Salter's girlfriend, who was traveling with Salter and Head at the time of the robbery, the two criminals had spent the last five months traveling up and down the East Coast. While Salter hid from the FBI, he supported himself by robbing banks and jewelry stores.

• • •

December 2, 1994, fell on a Friday. In a small cluster of stores lining a highway several miles from downtown Richmond, Gary Baker opened his shop promptly at 10:00 A.M. Outside Beverly Hills Jewelers, wreaths of mistletoe decorated the streetlights, a cheery reminder that the Christmas season was in full swing.

Traditionally, December is a jeweler's most profitable month, and Baker was optimistic as he stepped up to his platform office in the back of his store. Once he settled in at his desk, he grabbed a cup of coffee and plunged into his paperwork.

When he next looked up, at about 10:15, two men wearing ski masks walked into the store. One stayed near the front door, while the other walked straight toward the back office pulling a suitcase on wheels.

Baker reached for a pistol and stood up. As the masked man approached the back counter, he stopped and looked up at Baker. The steel-blue eyes of both men locked for a few tense, pulse-pounding seconds. Briefly, Baker wondered if this was just a stupid joke. The answer came when the ski-masked robber vaulted onto the wooden counter.

"He was in very, very good shape," Baker said afterward. "He was on top of the work counter in a flash."

The robber straightened up, and Baker could see that he was massive and muscular. Baker spotted his .45 the same instant the gunman saw Baker's .38.

Baker recalled, "The second robber, armed with a sawed-off shotgun, stood five or six feet inside the front door. I assume his job was to make sure nobody got out alive, and if a customer should walk in, he'd take care of them.

"Three employees were now down on the floor, armed and pushing holdup buttons as previously trained."

As soon as the robber with the .45 stood up on the counter, the second assailant fired. The concussion from his sawed-off shotgun rocked the showroom.

At that point, Baker recalled, the wondering was over and all hell broke loose.

"An employee and I immediately fired on the guy coming over the counter. My .38 went BOOM BOOM BOOM.

"I saw him falling forward on our side of the counter. But because I'm on a raised platform and I had a wall in front of me, I didn't see him hit the floor."

The first assailant to go down was hit a total of seven times. As he lay on his back, one of his legs kicked out spasmodically and came to rest on a desk.

"As soon as the first robber fell, I was looking at the second gunman behind him," Baker recalled. "It's a straight line from where I'm sitting to the front door. The guy with the shotgun was now moving toward me. As soon as one goes down, here comes the next guy."

Baker fired his .38 twice more. The second robber leaped behind the center showcase where Baker couldn't see him.

"I've been hit!" the assailant shouted.

Baker remembered, "One of my employees yelled for him to throw his gun out and he replied, 'I am, I am!' Everything stopped for a few seconds. This turned out to be a stalling ploy as the robber reloaded his shotgun and fired again.

"I still don't know who he was shooting at. But when somebody shoots a shotgun in your direction, it always looks like its coming at you. That's when I was hit. It was a ricochet, I think."

Baker was struck in the left hand. Blood pooled inside his hand, but he continued to focus on the second gunman.

"At that point," he said, "I turned around and picked up my shotgun. I had double-ought buckshot, which is what he also turned out to be shooting. But his shotgun was sawed off to an extremely short length, which may be why he never killed anybody. I aimed at where I thought he was and waited for him to come back up. When he popped up to shoot again, he was right in my line of fire."

Baker pulled the trigger and felt the shock of the recoil as the twelve-gauge exploded. William "Pappy" Head's long life of violence came to an end.

Everything went graveyard silent as the scales of justice dipped briefly on the side of righteousness.

By the time the police arrived, the windows of the store were riddled with bullets, and smoke was oozing out of the holes. As they looked inside, the officers couldn't help but gasp. Gary Baker stood in suit and tie, holding a smoking shotgun over the ski-masked robber as the cops entered the store.

The first policeman asked for Baker's weapon, and others ushered his employees outside. They were immediately separated to be interrogated by detectives. Baker's lawyer arrived and urged him not to talk. But the store owner felt he had nothing to hide and encouraged his employees to fully cooperate with police.

Baker's hand continued to bleed steadily. He allowed it to be bandaged by medics, but he refused to go to the hospital. His only concern was to call his wife and four children and tell them that he and his employees were all safe.

The police department had a difficult time identifying the robbers. Neither had a driver's license or other identification. An automobile left running and parked beside the jewelry store proved to have been stolen.

When their fingerprints were finally run through the FBI computer, local authorities were stunned to learn that their long, violent, criminal histories rivaled those of Frank and Jesse James.

William Lawrence "Pappy" Head was so well known in Texas that Hardin County, Texas, sheriff Mike Holzapfel called the *Richmond Times-Dispatch* just to confirm that he was dead.

Holzapfel explained, "The Dixie Mafia's not as organized as it once was, but it's still down here."

In his fifty-five years of criminal activity, Pappy Head had robbed dozens of banks and jewelry stores. He'd also committed scores of big-time burglaries and smuggled tons of marijuana in from Mexico.

Head also murdered people. After the execution murder of Weldon Fossey, Sheriff Holzapfel began compiling a thick dossier on Head and his cronies.

"When that Mississippi judge got killed," Holzapfel said, "the Mafia boys deserted Biloxi, which had been their headquarters.

Southern Florida became their new meeting place. Head and his cronies forged ties with transient carnival people, who they'd get to peddle their dope all over the U.S."

Holzapfel speculated that Head had met his last partner, Thomas Jefferson Salter, in Miami at one of the annual crime conventions. He believes that Head would have had no qualms in killing the jewelry store employees. But all's well that ends well, Holzapfel concluded. "Pappy Head died the way he was supposed to die."

For Gary Baker, the public response was overwhelmingly positive. Cards and letters from Florida to Canada flooded his mailbox. Bill McIntire, a spokesperson for the National Rifle Association, said, "A potential disaster was averted because Baker and his employees knew what to do and when to do it." Virginia Governor George Allen said he joined in the widespread support of Baker. "I think the reason there's a great deal of sentiment in support of these folks at this particular store is that for once, the victims fought back and the good guys won."

Radio talk show host G. Gordon Liddy proclaimed that Baker should be given a medal. Columnists of the *Richmond Times-Dispatch* lavishly praised his actions. Cards and letters from Florida to Canada flooded his mailbox, and strangers called to congratulate him.

• • •

On January 25, 1995, Gary Baker appeared before the Virginia Senate Courts of Justice Committee to testify in favor of the state's "right-to-carry" legislation.

In his testimony, he stated, "I am deeply troubled by the Virginia Legislature's failure to provide equal protection under the law for all law-abiding citizens of Virginia. Department of Justice statistics indicate that 87 percent of all violent crimes occur outside the home. However, in many counties in Virginia, citizens are unable to carry a firearm for self-defense outside their home due to the distortion and misinterpretation of the current right-to-carry system. With the reform of the right-to-carry system in Virginia, all citizens will have an equal opportunity to exercise their rights."

Baker's testimony helped sway legislators to pass a comprehensive right-to-carry law for the state of Virginia. In late 1995, Governor George Allen signed it into law. On March 31, 1995, Baker also testified before the United States House of Representatives Subcommittee on Crime in Washington, D.C. He supported an attempt to repeal the ban on certain types of automatic weapons that has, tragically, resulted in criminals being better armed than law-abiding citizens and the police on the streets.

Baker has spent the last several years analyzing crime, criminals, and the police response to criminal activity.

Thinking back on the incident, he said, "One thing I realized after the attempted robbery is the false security a lot of people have with these holdup buttons. If we hadn't fought back and had only pushed the holdup buttons, we would have become hostages. The police got here within seconds of the gunfight.

"You're talking about violent career criminals who would never see the light of day again with their backgrounds. This three-strikes-and-you're-out stuff, well, these guys were long past that. I wouldn't have wanted those vicious killers holding guns to my head and the police trying to negotiate them out. They would have no reason not to kill you.

"Holdup buttons and video cameras might help the police solve murders, but that wouldn't have helped me or my employees any."

In referring to the response of Henrico County police, Baker said, "Let's give the police credit. They were extremely nice and very understanding. Never at any point did I feel intimidated or threatened by them. In fact, it was just the opposite.

"I could tell the policemen on the street and those that were guarding the door thought what had happened was terrific. They smiled, winked, and flashed thumbs-up to let me know they approved of my defensive actions. Of course, the brass was around so they couldn't actually say much.

"Most police chiefs tell citizens not to resist armed robberies. Most sheriffs tell you to fight back. The difference between the two is the police chief is appointed by politicians and says whatever happens to be politically correct. Sheriffs are elected by the people, so they are more inclined to tell you the truth."

Although Baker does not belong to the National Rifle Association, he strongly supports its causes on behalf of the rights of law-abiding gun owners.

"I called the NRA to thank them for standing up for my Second Amendment rights. Their efforts enabled me and my employees to survive this savage attack. Americans must come to realize that if guns are outlawed, only outlaws will have guns."

Speaking of criminals, Baker continued, "In general, they are total failures in most of life's normal activities, such as school, work, marriage, and fatherhood. Their failures are at a tremendous burden and economic cost to society. The only thing these losers seem successful at is being a criminal. And the only reason for that is—we the people—allow it to happen.

"But times they are a-changing. There was a time when the police were telling women, if you are accosted in a parking lot by a man with a knife or a gun, do what he tells you. Get in the car if he tells you to and hopefully he won't do much more than rob you. Only God knows how many women were brutally raped and murdered after heeding that lie.

"Now they're finally telling women the truth. They're saying, 'If you get in that car, you're dead! Fight back, run, scream, faint, or do whatever, but don't get in that car!'

"The advice most police departments are now giving the public about not fighting back with guns is suicidal. Why shouldn't people who are successful in life be able to prevail over those who are unsuccessful in everything they've ever done in their lives? Why shouldn't we have an advantage? We're smarter, we can easily become better trained, and we have our choice of weapons. Criminals don't. Their choice of weapons is whatever they happen to steal."

Speaking of that day in December 1994, Baker said simply, "I'm glad I chose to take personal responsibility for the safety of my employees, customers, and myself. Hoping the cavalry will ride to your rescue is just a silly fairy tale. Our government must never be allowed to disarm law-abiding citizens."

Afterword

Writing this book has been a humbling experience. The majority of those individuals whom I contacted were willing to sit for long interviews reliving violent and emotional experiences. They had riveting stories to tell, accounts of cold, stark terror and steel courage.

I have taken great pains to make each story as accurate as possible. In addition to taped interviews from would-be victims who fought back, I read police reports, newspaper accounts, court documents, internal office memos (as in the case of the Potts Camp bank robbery in which the would-be victim wrote an account of his actions for his superiors), and additional records that ensure the accuracy of each story.

While writing these stories, I felt a sense of duty to each individual who told his or her story. It was important to me to present a factual account of what happened. If there is drama involved, the events themselves provided it.

In a few instances, when quoting from tape recordings, I have placed events in a slightly different order. However, I have not deviated in any way from the meaning of the statements given me.

As in all human events, conflicting interpretations are occasionally presented, such as in a police report made by a law enforcement official versus the taped statement of a would-be victim. I have attempted, in those cases, to come to the most logical conclusion possible, and to present it as such.

As mentioned earlier, I did not write this book to enter the gun control debate. While my personal opinion is that law-abiding citizens should have the right to own weapons, the availability of guns, especially to children and persons with violent criminal histories, is troubling. It is particularly distressing to see young people injured or killed when playing with guns. I would favor any sane attempt to eliminate such deaths and injuries, while maintaining the right to own and use firearms.

Many of the individuals I talked with would undoubtedly be dead or severely injured had they not had access to weapons. In the case of Doug Stanton, for instance, his attacker had already murdered four people, including a 5-month-old baby. Had Stanton not taken precautions to obtain weapons and train his family in what to do before they were attacked, there is little doubt that he, his wife, and four children would have been murdered.

Sammie Foust was half the size of her attacker. Even after shooting him four times, he was able to inflict horrendous injuries. She'd been beaten and cut so badly that the police, ambulance crew, and firefighters cheered when they discovered that her attacker was dead.

One of the things that stood out in my research was the number of repeat offenders who continue to be let out of prison to commit more violent acts. For example, the two career criminals who attacked Gary Baker and his employees at Beverly Hills Jewelers had almost a century of criminal activity between them. Armed robbery, burglary, kidnapping, assault, and murder were only a few of the charges they'd been convicted of. Such cases cry out for drastic change in a system that allows violent offenders to continually go free and victimize more people.

In another case, Demetreus Jerome Lowe had been arrested sixteen times in a three-year period before he and a companion attempted to rob Kenneth and Mary Ellen Moring. He'd served only a few weeks of jail time for all his arrests. Even though most of his previous charges were drug-related, he was obviously a menace and needed to be taken out of society.

Things may be improving. Citizen reaction to such violence has forced changes in some states, either through ballot initiatives or through legislative action.

For instance, the "three-strikes-and-you're-out" initiative passed in California in 1994. This was despite dire predictions—some would call them threats—from many politicians, media pundits, and criminologists that they would have to tax the population into poverty to build new prisons.

Sadly, the impetus for the initiative turned out to be a girls' slumber party. In October 1993, 12-year-old Polly Klaas was kidnapped at knifepoint from her own bedroom. It was a parent's worst nightmare, and the abduction struck a chord with most Americans.

When a violent repeat offender was arrested for the crime three months later, citizens were outraged. Timothy Allen Davis had been arrested dozens of times. He'd been convicted of violent sex crimes and kidnapping, as well as run-of-the-mill crimes such as robbery, burglary, and drug offenses. He'd just gained early release from prison where he'd served time for kidnapping. He was a predator of the worst sort, and people wondered how he could still be out on the streets.

A ballot initiative called "three-strikes-and-you're-out" was quickly drawn up, placed on the ballot, and passed by a whopping 73 percent to 27 percent. The law states that persons convicted of three or more felonies may end up facing life in prison.

The solution was obvious all along. Less than 1 percent of the population are repeat violent offenders. If they are taken off the streets for the rest of their lives, violent crime will decrease. Many states now have some form of the three-strikes-and-you're-out law, and the violent crime rate is going down.

In addition to locking away repeat violent offenders for long periods of time, our society must at some point confront the relationship between drug usage and violence. It may be symptomatic of where we stand as a nation when the President of the United States can make light of his own drug use on a network watched almost exclusively by young people, and when two states pass ballot initiatives legalizing the use of marijuana.

In more than three-quarters of the cases outlined in this book, there was a long history of drug abuse by the assailant. We're not living in the 1960s anymore. Drugs are not new and attractive and embalmed with the scent of "flower power." We know now that drugs, even marijuana, are addictive. Harder drugs, such as crack cocaine, obviously have a precipitating effect on violent behavior—otherwise, so many crack addicts would not be in our prisons and mental hospitals for violent offenses.

Many citizens favor stiff penalties for violation of drug laws. Some states seem to be slowly marching toward mandatory long-term sentences for individuals caught selling drugs. Such laws would certainly get some violent offenders off the streets.

We come back to guns.

Should weapons be banned? Again, the truth seems obvious. In thousands of cases each year, law-abiding citizens use firearms to protect themselves, their families, and even strangers from violent attacks. These citizens should, as is guaranteed by our constitution, have a right to possess guns.

Mandatory life in prison for anyone who commits a felony with a firearm would have an immediate impact on violent crime. In addition, a sure and certain death penalty for anyone who takes a life while committing a felony with a firearm would drastically reduce such crimes.

The people I interviewed have no uncertainty about their beliefs. They feel that they have the right to protect themselves and others, and that guns are the best defense.

Many would-be victims struggle with guilt. Even though they know they did what was necessary to survive, their emotions will not let their experiences be so black and white. Many tears were shed during these interviews: tears for "some mother's son," as Sammie Foust put it; tears of rage at being put in a position of having to take a life; tears of gratitude for surviving a brutal attack.

Others have no remorse at all. They feel that their assailants made a choice—when they became criminals, they accepted the risks that go with that occupation. As Gary B. Baker said, "I have four children and a wife, and it gets me mad thinking about people trying to take my life away from me."

The conclusion I reached was that Americans place a high value on human life: their own lives, the lives of their families, their employees, strangers, even the lives of their assailants. In more than one case, the would-be victim shot in the air to scare off his attacker, rather than to kill him.

The stereotypical shoot-from-the-hip redneck doesn't apply in the cases I've presented. None are members of any militia. None are vigilantes. All are citizens who were going about their daily activities when they were attacked.

Many had thought out ahead of time what situations would call for the use of a firearm. In most cases, they were surprised that the situation arose. Whether it was tightening a business with the greatest security possible or merely going over in one's mind what circumstances would dictate the use of deadly force, most of those I interviewed had a game plan. Gary B. Baker said it cogently, "The police are a reactionary force. They only react after a crime. So it's up to the individual to protect himself or herself."

For this reason, those I interviewed favored keeping weapons available to law-abiding citizens. Most know that political gradualism will eventually conspire to ban all firearms if allowed to build a head of steam.

They also know that without access to a weapon, they might not have been alive to give the interview that I requested.

About the Author

Robert A. Waters is former director of adult programs for an association of retarded adults and former counselor in the departments of vocational rehabilitation in Tennessee and Florida. Now living in Ocala, Florida, he has written numerous articles about collectibles in magazines and newsletters. *The Best Defense* is his first book.

Photo by Sim Waters